RESEARCHES

INTO THE

MATHEMATICAL PRINCIPLES

OF THE

THEORY OF WEALTH

BY

AUGUSTIN COURNOT

1838

TRANSLATED BY NATHANIEL T. BACON

WITH A

BIBLIOGRAPHY OF MATHEMATICAL ECONOMICS

BY IRVING FISHER

New York

THE MACMILLAN COMPANY

LONDON: MACMILLAN & CO., LTD.

1897

COPYRIGHT, 1897,
BY THE MACMILLAN COMPANY.

Norwood Press
J. S. Cushing & Co. — Berwick & Smith
Norwood Mass. U.S.A.

ANTOINE AUGUSTIN COURNOT was born at Gray, in Haute-Saône, France, on Aug. 28, 1801. He received his early schooling in his native town, and his first special discipline in mathematics at the Lycée de Besançon. In 1821 he entered the École Normale at Paris, where he continued his mathematical studies. He became Professor of Mathematics at Lyons in 1834, and the year following Rector of the Academy at Grenoble. In 1838 appeared his *Recherches sur les principes mathématiques de la théorie des richesses*, of which the present work is a translation. In the same year Cournot was called to Paris as Inspecteur Général des Études. He was made Knight of the Legion of Honour in 1838, and Officer in 1845. He became Rector of the Academy at Dijon in 1854, but in 1862 retired from active teaching. From this time to the end of his life he was busily engaged in writing. His *Principes mathématiques* having met with little or no success, in 1863 he paraphrased it in popular language under the title *Principes de la théorie des richesses*, which was further amplified in 1876 as *Revue sommaire des doctrines économiques*. He died in the following year, on March 31, in Paris.

Among Cournot's mathematical writings may be mentioned his *Traité élémentaire de la théorie des fonctions et du calcul infinitésimal*, 1841 ; *De l'origine et des limites de la correspondence entre l'algèbre et la géométrie*, 1847 ; and *Exposition de la théorie des chances et des probabilités*, 1843. In the last-named work he showed how to apply the theory of chances to Statistics.

Cournot also produced several philosophical works, *e.g* *Traité de l'enchainement des idées fondamentales dans les sciences et dans l'histoire*, 1861 ; and *Considérations sur la marche des idées et des événements dans les temps modernes*, 1872. He also translated some English mathematical books, including Sir John Herschel's *Astronomy*, and edited in two volumes Euler's celebrated *Letters to a Princess*, etc.

For the facts of Cournot's life see Liard, *Revue des Deux Mondes*, July, 1877 ; and *Nouvelle Biographie Générale*. For criticisms of his work in economics see Palgrave's *Dictionary of Political Economy;* and the prefaces of Jevons's *Theory of Political Economy* (second edition), Walras's *Éléments d'économie politique pure*, Auspitz and Lieben's *Untersuchungen über die Theorie des Preises*, and Marshall's *Principles of Economics ;* also an article by Vilfredo Pareto, *Di un errore del Cournot nel trattare l'economia politica colla matematica*, in the *Giornale degli economisti*, January, 1892, and one by Edgeworth, *La teoria pura del monopolio, ibid.*, July, 1897. The present writer will shortly publish in the *Quarterly Journal of Economics* an article critical and explanatory of the *Principes mathématiques*, and intended especially for the use of those who may wish to follow the reasoning of the work in detail, but lack the requisite familiarity with mathematics. He is also preparing a brief Introduction to the Calculus for a similar purpose.

In rendering the book into English, the translator (Mr. Nathaniel T. Bacon, of Peacedale, R.I. ; Ph.B., Yale, 1879) has tried to be as literal as possible, and to retain the slight archaism of the French. He has also followed out the mathematical operations with great care, and in so doing discovered a surprisingly large number of errors. Most of these were misprints ; others were due to obvious carelessness of the author, while still others were doubtful as to their origin. All have been corrected except two, which were the only ones seriously affecting the argument. These are formulæ (6) on page 122, and the next but last inequality on page 158. The true formulæ may be transcribed from (6), page 122, by substituting zero for ϵ; and the inequality on page 158 may be corrected by reversing the sign of inequality. The conclusions which follow each passage must be materially modified.

For nearly forty years the *Principes mathématiques* was completely ignored by economists. The writers chiefly instrumental in reviving the work were Jevons, Walras, and Boccardo. At present, though mathematico-economic works are not yet widely read, Cournot's treatise is diligently studied by a few, and exercises a very definite and powerful influence on economic thought. Professor Edgeworth says of it in Palgrave's *Dictionary*, that it " is still the best statement in mathematical form of some of the highest generalisations in economic science " ; while Professor Marshall, in the preface to his *Principles*, declares that " Cournot's genius must give a new mental activity to every one who passes through his hands."

The bibliography of mathematical economics is, of course, founded on that appended to Jevons's *Theory of Political Economy*. A number of writings in the latter list have been omitted, as they did not make use of symbols. Even the *Volkswirthschaftslehre* of Menger, who shares with Jevons and Walras the honour of independently developing the theory of marginal utility, has not been included, as it must properly be credited to the literary and not the mathematical method. Jevons's list has also been carefully revised and corrected, as well as continued to 1897.

The bibliography divides itself very naturally into four periods, beginning respectively with the treatises of Ceva, Cournot, Jevons, and Marshall. Ceva enjoys the distinction of being the first known writer to apply mathematical method to economic problems; Cournot was apparently the first to apply it with any great degree of success; Jevons (and almost simultaneously Walras) attracted the serious attention of economists to this method; and Marshall brought it (or at any rate its simpler diagrams) into general use. The four periods are of constantly decreasing length, being respectively 127, 33, 19, and 8 years, but the number of titles grows greater in each succeeding period. It will also be observed that the variety of subjects to which the mathematical method is being applied shows a rapid increase, that the number of complete economic treatises has grown relatively less, and that the mass of literature on transportation has first risen and then fallen relatively to the total writing.

In preparing the work for the press, important aid has been rendered by Mr. John M. Gaines, of the graduate department of Yale University. Mr. Thomas G. Barnes, Mr. James O. Moore, and especially Mr. William B. Bailey, also students at Yale, have contributed materially in the formation of the bibliography. Grateful acknowledgments are due to the many other persons who have supplied bibliographical data, and in particular to Professors Pantaleoni, Walras, Pareto, and Edgeworth.

I. F.

CONTENTS

ix

PREFACE

———◦◦◦———

THE science known as Political Economy, which for a
century has so much interested thinkers, is to-day more
generally diffused than ever before. It shares with politics
proper the attention of the great journals, which are to-day
the most important means of spreading information; but
the public is so tired of theories and systems that now the
demand is for so-called "positive" matter, *i.e.* in political
economy, custom-house abstracts, statistical documents, and
government reports, such as will throw the light of experience on the important questions which are being agitated
before the country, and which so greatly interest all classes
of society.

I make no objection to this tendency; it is good, and
in accord with the laws which govern the development of
all branches of science. I will only observe that *theory*
ought not to be confounded with systems, although in
the infancy of all sciences the instinct of system necessarily attempts to outline theories. I will add that theory
should always have some part, small though it may be,
in the development of a science; and that, to a man of my
profession in particular, more than to any other, it should
be permissible to consider from an exclusively theoretical

standpoint, a subject of general interest which has so many different sides.

But the title of this work sets forth not only theoretical researches; it shows also that I intend to apply to them the forms and symbols of mathematical analysis. This is a plan likely, I confess, to draw on me at the outset the condemnation of theorists of repute. With one accord they have set themselves against the use of mathematical forms, and it will doubtless be difficult to overcome to-day a prejudice which thinkers, like Smith and other more modern writers, have contributed to strengthen. The reasons for this prejudice seem to be, on the one hand, the false point of view from which theory has been regarded by the small number of those who have thought of applying mathematics to it; and, on the other hand, the false notion which has been formed of this analysis by men otherwise judicious and well versed in the subject of Political Economy, but to whom the mathematical sciences are unfamiliar.

The attempts which have been made in this direction have remained very little known, and I have been able to learn only the titles of them, except one, *Les Principes de l'Économie Politique*, by *Canard*, a small work published in the year X [of the French Republic, A.D. 1801], and crowned by the *Institut*. These pretended principles are so radically at fault, and the application of them is so erroneous, that the approval of a distinguished body of men was unable to preserve the work from oblivion. It is easy to see why essays of this nature should not incline such economists as Say and Ricardo to algebra.

I have said that most authors who have devoted them-

selves to political economy seem also to have had a wrong
idea of the nature of the applications of mathematical
analysis to the theory of wealth. They imagined that the
use of symbols and formulas could only lead to numerical
calculations, and as it was clearly perceived that the subject was not suited to such a numerical determination of
values by means of theory alone, the conclusion was drawn
that the mathematical apparatus, if not liable to lead to
erroneous results, was at least idle and pedantic. But those
skilled in mathematical analysis know that its object is not
simply to calculate numbers, but that it is also employed to
find the relations between magnitudes which cannot be expressed in numbers and between *functions* whose law is not
capable of algebraic expression. Thus the theory of prob-
abilities furnishes a demonstration of very important propo-
sitions, although, without the help of experience, it is
impossible to give numerical values for contingent events,
except in questions of mere curiosity, such as arise from
certain games of chance. Thus, also, theoretical Mechanics
furnishes to practical Mechanics general theorems of most
useful application, although in almost all cases recourse to
experience is necessary for the numerical results which
practice requires.

The employment of mathematical symbols is perfectly
natural when the relations between magnitudes are under
discussion ; and even if they are not rigorously necessary, it
would hardly be reasonable to reject them, because they
are not equally familiar to all readers and because they have
sometimes been wrongly used, if they are able to facilitate
the exposition of problems, to render it more concise, to

open the way to more extended developments, and to avoid the digressions of vague argumentation.

There are authors, like Smith and Say, who, in writing on Political Economy, have preserved all the beauties of a purely literary style ; but there are others, like Ricardo, who, when treating the most abstract questions, or when seeking great accuracy, have not been able to avoid algebra, and have only disguised it under arithmetical calculations of tiresome length. Any one who understands algebraic nota-tion, reads at a glance in an equation results reached arith-metically only with great labour and pains.

I propose to show in this essay that the solution of the general questions which arise from the theory of wealth, depends essentially not on elementary algebra, but on that branch of analysis which comprises arbitrary functions, which are merely restricted to satisfying certain conditions. As only very simple conditions will be considered, the first principles of the differential and integral calculus suffice for understanding this little treatise. Also, although I fear that it may appear too abstruse to most people who have a liking for these topics, I hardly dare to hope that it will deserve the attention of professional mathematicians, except as they may discover in it the germ of questions more worthy of their powers.

But there is a large class of men, and, thanks to a famous school, especially in France, who, after thorough mathe-matical training, have directed their attention to applica-tions of those sciences which particularly interest society. Theories of the wealth of the community must attract their attention ; and in considering them they are sure to feel, as

I have felt, the need of rendering determinate by symbols familiar to them, an analysis which is generally indeterminate and often obscure, in authors who have thought fit to confine themselves to the resources of ordinary language. In thinking that they may be led by their reflexions to enter upon this path, I hope that my book may be of some use to them, and may lessen their labour.

In the remarks on the first notions of competition and the mutual relations of producers, they may possibly notice certain relations, which are very curious from a purely abstract standpoint, without reference to proposed applications.

I have not set out to make a complete and dogmatic treatise on Political Economy; I have put aside questions, to which mathematical analysis cannot apply, and those which seem to me entirely cleared up already. I have assumed that this book will only fall into the hands of readers who are familiar with what is found in the most ordinary books on these topics.

I am far from having thought of writing in support of any system, and from joining the banners of any party; I believe that there is an immense step in passing from theory to governmental applications; I believe that theory loses none of its value in thus remaining preserved from contact with impassioned polemics; and I believe, if this essay is of any practical value, it will be chiefly in making clear how far we are from being able to solve, with full knowledge of the case, a multitude of questions which are boldly decided every day.

RESEARCHES

INTO

THE MATHEMATICAL PRINCIPLES

OF

THE THEORY OF WEALTH

———o○◦●◦○o———

CHAPTER I

OF VALUE IN EXCHANGE OR OF WEALTH IN GENERAL

1. The Teutonic root *Rik* or *Reich*, which has passed into all the Romance languages, vaguely expressed a relation of superiority, of strength, or of power. *Los ricos hombres* is still used in Spain for distinguished noblemen and eminent men, and such is also the force of the words *riches hommes* in the French of de Joinville. The idea which the word *wealth* presents to us to-day, and which is relative to our state of civilization, could not have been grasped by men of Teutonic stock, either at the epoch of the Conquest, or even at much later periods, when the feudal law existed in full vigour. Property, power, the distinctions between masters, servants and slaves, abundance, and poverty, rights and privileges, all these are found among the most savage tribes, and seem to flow necessarily from the natural laws which preside over aggregations

of individuals and of families ; but such an idea of wealth as we draw from our advanced state of civilization, and such as is necessary to give rise to a theory, can only be slowly developed as a consequence of the progress of commercial relations, and of the gradual reaction of those relations on civil institutions.

A shepherd is in possession of a vast pasture ground, and no one can disturb him with impunity ; but it would be vain for him to think of exchanging it for something which he might prefer ; there is nothing in existing habits and customs to make such an exchange possible ; this man is a landholder, but he is not rich.

The same shepherd has cattle and milk in abundance ; he can provide for a numerous retinue of servants and slaves ; he maintains a generous hospitality towards poor dependents ; but he is neither able to accumulate his products, nor to exchange them for objects of luxury which do not exist ; this man has power, authority, the enjoyments which belong to his position, but he has not wealth.

2. It is inconceivable that men should live for a considerable time near together without effecting an exchange of goods and services ; but from this natural, and we may even say instinctive, action, it is a long step to the abstract idea of *value in exchange*, which supposes that the objects to which such value is attributed *are in commercial circulation;* *i.e.* that it is always possible to find means to exchange them for other objects of equal value. The things, then, to which the state of commercial relations and civil institutions permits a value in exchange to be attached, are those which in the language of to-day are characterized by the word

wealth; and to form an intelligible theory we ought to absolutely identify the sense of the word *wealth* with that which is presented to us by the words *exchangeable values.*

Under this conception, *wealth* has doubtless only an abstract existence ; for, strictly speaking, of all the things on which we set a price, or to which we attribute a value in exchange, there are none always exchangeable at will for any other commodity of equal price or value. In the act of exchange, as in the transmission of power by machinery, there is friction to be overcome, losses which must be borne, and limits which cannot be exceeded. The proprietor of a great forest is only rich on condition of managing his lumbering with prudence, and of not glutting the market with his lumber ; the owner of a valuable picture gallery may spend his life in the vain attempt to find purchasers ; while, on the other hand, in the neighbourhood of a city the conversion of a sack of grain into money will only require the time necessary to carry it to the grain market ; and at great commercial centres a stock of coffee can always be sold on the exchange.

The extension of commerce and the development of commercial facilities tend to bring the actual condition of affairs nearer and nearer to this order of abstract conceptions, on which alone theoretical calculations can be based, in the same way as the skilful engineer approaches nearer to theoretical conditions by diminishing friction through polished bearings and accurate gearing. In this way nations are said to make progress in the commercial or mercantile system. These two expressions are etymologically equivalent, but one is now taken in a good and the other in a bad sense, as is generally the case, according to Bentham, with the names of things that involve advantages and evils of a moral order.

We will not take up either these advantages or these evils.
The progress of nations in the commercial system is a fact
in the face of which all discussion of its desirability becomes
idle ; our part is to observe, and not to criticise, the irre-
sistible laws of nature. Whatever man can measure, calculate, and systematize, ultimately becomes the object of measurement, calculation, and system. Wherever fixed relations
can replace indeterminate, the substitution finally takes place.
It is thus that the sciences and all human institutions are
organized. The use of coin, which has been handed down
to us from remote antiquity, has powerfully aided the
progress of commercial organization, as the art of making
glass helped many discoveries in astronomy and physics ;
but commercial organization is not essentially bound to the
use of the monetary metals. All means are good which
tend to facilitate exchange, to fix value in exchange ; and
there is reason to believe that in the further development
of this organization the monetary metals will play a part of
gradually diminishing importance.

3. The abstract idea of *wealth* or of *value in exchange*, a
definite idea, and consequently susceptible of rigorous treat-
ment in combinations, must be carefully distinguished from
the accessory ideas of utility, scarcity, and suitability to the
needs and enjoyments of mankind, which the word *wealth*
still suggests in common speech. These ideas are variable,
and by nature indeterminate, and consequently ill suited for
the foundation of a scientific theory. The division of economists into schools, and the war waged between practical
men and theorists, have arisen in large measure from the
ambiguity of the word *wealth* in ordinary speech, and the

confusion which has continued to obtain between the fixed, definite idea of *value in exchange*, and the ideas of utility which every one estimates in his own way, because there is no fixed standard for the utility of things.*

It has sometimes happened that a publisher, having in store an unsalable stock of some work, useful and sought after by connoisseurs, but of which too many copies were originally printed in view of the class of readers for whom it was intended, has sacrificed and destroyed two-thirds of the number, expecting to derive more profit from the remainder than from the entire edition.†

There is no doubt that there might be a book of which it would be easier to sell a thousand copies at sixty francs, than three thousand at twenty francs. Calculating in this way, the Dutch Company is said to have caused the destruction in the islands of the Sound of a part of the precious spices of which it had a monopoly. Here is a complete destruction of objects to which the word *wealth* is applied because they are both sought after, and not easily obtainable. Here is a miserly, selfish act, evidently opposed to the interests of society ; and yet it is nevertheless evident that this sordid act, this actual destruction, is a real creation of *wealth* in the commercial sense of the word. The

* By this we do not intend that there is neither truth nor error in opinions on the utility of things ; we only mean that generally neither the truth nor the error is capable of proof ; that these are questions of valuation, and not soluble by calculation, nor by logical argument.

† I have heard it said by a very respectable surveyor, that one of the greatest griefs which he had felt in his youth had been to learn that the publisher Dupont had done thus with the valuable collection of the Memoirs of the old Academy of Sciences.

publisher's inventory will rightly show a greater value for his assets ; and after the copies have left his hands, either wholly· or in part, if each individual should draw up his inventory in commercial fashion, and if all these partial inventories could be collated to form a general inventory or balance sheet of the wealth in circulation, an increase would be found in the sum of these items of wealth.

On the contrary, suppose that only fifty copies exist of a curious book, and that this scarcity carries up the price at auction to three hundred francs a copy. A publisher re-prints this book in an edition of a thousand copies, of which each will be worth five francs, and which will bring down the other copies to the same price from the exaggerated value which their extreme scarcity had caused. The 1050 copies will therefore only enter for 5250 francs into the sum of wealth which can be inventoried, and this sum will thus have suffered a loss of 9750 francs. The decrease will be even more considerable if (as should be the case) the value of the raw materials is considered, from which the reprints were made, and which existed prior to the reprinting. Here is an industrial operation, a material production, use-ful to the publisher who undertook it, useful to those whose products and labour it employed, useful even to the public if the book contains valuable information, and which is nevertheless a real destruction of wealth, in the abstract and commercial meaning of the term.

The rise and fall of exchange show perpetual oscillations in values, or in the abstract wealth in circulation, without intervention of actual production or destruction of the phys-ical objects to which, in the concrete sense, the term *wealth* is applicable.

It has been long remarked, and justly, that commerce, properly so called, *i.e.* the transportation of raw materials or finished products, from one market to another, by adding to the worth of the objects transported, creates value or wealth in just the same way as the labour of the miner who extracts metals from the bowels of the earth, or the workman who adapts them to our needs. What ought to have been added, and what we shall have occasion to develop, is that commerce may also be a cause of destruction of values, even while making profits for the merchants who carry it on, and even when in every one's eyes it is a benefit to the countries which it connects in commercial intercourse.

A fashion, a whim, or a chance occurrence may cause a creation or annihilation of values without notable influence on what is regarded as public utility or the general welfare ; it can even come about that a destruction of wealth may be salutary, and an increase detrimental. If chemists should solve the problem of making diamonds, jewellers and the ladies who own sets of jewellery would suffer heavy losses ; the general mass of wealth capable of circulation would experience a notable decrease, and yet I can hardly think than any sensible man would be tempted to consider it a public calamity, even though he might regret the individual losses involved. On the contrary, if the taste for diamonds should decline, if wealthy people should stop devoting an important part of their fortunes to this idle vanity, and if, in consequence, the value of diamonds in commerce should decrease, wise men would gladly commend this new departure of fashion.

4. When any event, accounted favourable to a country, as improving the condition of the majority of its inhabitants (for what other basis can be taken to estimate utility?), has nevertheless for its first effect the diminution of the mass of values in circulation, we are tempted to suppose that this event conceals the germ of an increase in the general wealth by means of its remote consequences, and that it will in this way turn out to the advantage of the country. Experience unquestionably shows that this is true in most cases, since, in general, an incontestable improvement in the condition of the people has kept pace with an equally incontestable increase in the sum total of wealth in circulation. But in consequence of the impossibility of following up analytically all the consequences of such complex relations, theory is unable to explain why this usually happens and is still less able to demonstrate that it must always continue to occur. Let us avoid confounding what is in the domain of accurate reasoning with what is the object of a more or less happy guess; what is rational with what is empirical. It is enough to have to guard against errors in logic on the first score; let us avoid encountering passionate declamations and insoluble questions on the other.

5. From a standpoint of mere etymology, whatever appertains to the organization of society belongs to the field of Political Economy; but it has become customary to use this last term in a sense much more restricted and by so much less precise. The Political Economist, being occupied principally with the material wants of mankind, only considers social institutions as far as they favour or interfere with labour, thrift, commerce, and population; and as far as they

affect the subdivision between the members of society of the gifts of nature and the rewards of labour.

This subject is still far too vast to be properly grasped by any one man. It affords inexhaustible material for unripe systems and slow investigations. How can we abstract the moral influences which enter into all these questions and which are entirely incapable of measurement? How are we to compare what may be called the material welfare of the Alpine shepherd with that of the Spanish idler or of the Manchester workingman; the convent alms with the poor-rates; the drudgery of the farm with that of the workshop; the pleasures and expenditures of a Norman noble in his feudal manor, with the pleasures and expenditures of his far-away descendant in a house in London or on a tour through Europe?

If we compare one nation with another, by what invariable tokens shall we determine the progress or decay of their prosperity? Shall it be according to population? In that case China would far excel Europe. According to the abundance of coin? The example of Spain, mistress of the Peruvian mines, turned the world away from this gross error long ago, and, in fact, before even the first crude notions of the true rôle of coin were developed. According to business activity? Then inland peoples would be very unfortunate compared with those whom proximity to the sea invites to a mercantile career. According to the high price of goods or of wages? Then some miserable island would surpass the most smiling and fertile countries. According to the pecuniary value of what economists call the annual product? A year when this value increases greatly may easily be one of great distress for the greatest number.

According to the actual quantity of this product reckoned in the appropriate unit for each kind of goods? But the kinds of goods produced and the relative proportions are different for each country. How can comparisons be made in this respect? According to the rate of movement up or down whether of population or of annual product? Provided that the reckoning covers a sufficient time this is, to be sure, the least equivocal symptom of the welfare or misery of society ; but how can this symptom help us except to recognize accomplished facts, and facts which have been produced, not only by economic causes in the ordinary meaning of the words, but also by the simultaneous coöperation of a multitude of moral causes.

We are far from wishing to depreciate the philanthropic efforts of those who seek to throw some light on social economy. It is characteristic only of narrow minds to decry medical science because physiological phenomena cannot be calculated as accurately as the planetary movements. Political Economy is the hygiene and pathology of the social system. It recognizes as its guide experience or rather observation ; but sometimes the sagacity of a superior mind can even anticipate the results of experience. We only seek to make clear, that Political Economy fails to make progress by theory, towards its noble object of the improvement of the lot of mankind, either because the relations which it has to deal with are not reducible to fixed terms, or because these relations are much too complicated for our powers of combination and analysis.

6. On the other hand, as the abstract idea of wealth according to our conception constitutes a perfectly deter-

minate relation, like all precise conceptions it can become the object of theoretical deductions, and if these deductions are sufficiently numerous and seem important enough to be collected into a system, it will presumably be advantageous to present this system by itself, except for such applications as it may seem proper to make to those branches of Political Economy with which the theory of wealth is ultimately connected. It will be useful to distinguish what admits of abstract demonstration from what allows only of a questionable opinion.

The Theory of Wealth, according to the idea we are trying to give, would doubtless only be an idle speculation, if the abstract idea of *wealth* or *value in exchange*, on which it is founded, were too far from corresponding with the actual objects which make up wealth in the existing social status. The same would be true of hydrostatics if the character of ordinary fluids should be too far removed from the hypothesis of perfect fluidity. However, as we have already said, the influence of a progressive civilization constantly tends to bring actual and variable relations nearer and nearer to the absolute relation, which we attain to from abstract considerations. In such matters everything becomes more and more easily valued, and consequently more easily measured. The steps towards finding a market resolve themselves into brokerage, losses of time into discounts, chances of loss into insurance charges, and so on. The progress of the gregarious tendency and of the institutions related to it, and the modifications which have taken place in our civil institutions, all coöperate towards this mobility, which we would neither apologize for nor detract from, but on which the application of theory to social facts is founded.

c

CHAPTER II

OF CHANGES IN VALUE, ABSOLUTE AND RELATIVE

7. Whenever there is occasion to go back to the fundamental conceptions on which any science rests, and to formulate them with accuracy, we almost always encounter difficulties, which come, sometimes from the very nature of these conceptions, but more often from the imperfections of language. For instance, in the writings of economists, the definition of *value*, and the distinction between absolute and relative value, are rather obscure : a very simple and strikingly exact comparison will serve to throw light on this.

We conceive that a body moves when its situation changes with reference to other bodies which we look upon as fixed. If we observe a system of material points at two different times, and find that the respective situations of these points are not the same at both times, we necessarily conclude that some, if not all, of these points have moved ; but if besides this we are unable to refer them to points of the fixity of which we can be sure, it is, in the first instance, impossible to draw any conclusions as to the motion or rest of each of the points in the system.

However, if all of the points in the system, except one, had preserved their relative situation, we should consider it very probable that this single point was the only one which

had moved, unless, indeed, all the other points were so connected that the movement of one would involve the movement of all.

We have just pointed out an extreme case, viz., that in
which all except one had kept their relative positions ; but,
without entering into details, it is easy to see that among
all the possible ways of explaining the change in the state
of the system there may be some much simpler than others,
and which without hesitation we regard as much more
probable.

If, without being limited to two distinct times, observation should follow the system through its successive states,
there would be hypotheses as to the absolute movements of
the different points of the system, which would be considered preferable for the explanation of their relative movements.   Thus, without reference to the relative size of the
heavenly bodies and to knowledge of the laws of gravitation,
the hypothesis of Copernicus would explain the apparent
motions of the planetary system more simply and plausibly
than those of Ptolemy or Tycho.

In the preceding paragraph we have only looked on
motion as a geometric relation, a change of position, without reference to any idea of cause or motive power or any
knowledge of the laws which govern the movements of matter.   From this new point of view other considerations of
probability will arise.   If, for instance, the mass of the body
A is considerably greater than that of the body B, we judge
that the change in the relative situation of the bodies A and
B is more probably due to the displacement of B than
of A.

Finally, there are some circumstances which may make it
certain that relative or apparent movements come from the
displacement of one body and not of another.* Thus the
appearance of an animal will show by unmistakable signs
whether it is stopping or starting. Thus, to return to the
preceding example, experiments with the pendulum, taken
in connection with the known laws of mechanics, will prove
the diurnal motion of the earth ; the phenomenon of the
aberration of light will prove its annual motion ; and the
hypothesis of Copernicus will take its place among established truths.

8. Let us now examine how some considerations perfectly analogous to those which we have just considered,
spring from the idea of exchangeable values.

Just as we can only assign situation to a point by reference to other points, so we can only assign value to a
commodity † by reference to other commodities. In this
sense there are only relative values. But when these relative values change, we perceive plainly that the reason of the
variation may lie in the change of one term of the relation
or of the other or of both at once ; just as when the distance
varies between two points, the reason for the change may
lie in the displacement of one or the other or both of the

* See Newton, *Principia*, Book I, at the end of the preliminary defi-
nitions.

† It is almost needless to observe that for conciseness the word *commodity* is used in its most general sense, and that it includes the rendering
of valuable services, which can be exchanged either for other services or
for commodities proper, and which, like such commodities, have a definite
price or a value in exchange. We shall not repeat this remark in the future,
as it can easily be supplied from the context.

two points. Thus again when two violin strings have had
between them a definite musical interval, and when after a
certain time they cease to give this interval, the question
is whether one has gone up or the other gone down, or
whether both of these effects have joined to cause the variation of the interval.

We can therefore readily distinguish the relative changes
of value manifested by the changes of relative values from
the absolute changes of value of one or another of the commodities between which commerce has established relations.

Just as it is possible to make an indefinite number of
hypotheses as to the absolute motion which causes the
observed relative motion in a system of points, so it is
also possible to multiply indefinitely hypotheses as to the
absolute variations which cause the relative variations observed in the values of a system of commodities.

However, if all but one of the commodities preserved the
same relative values, we should consider by far the most
probable hypothesis, the one which would assign the absolute change to this single article ; unless there should be
manifest such a connection between all the others, that one
cannot vary without involving proportional variations in the
values of those which depend on it.

For instance, an observer who should see by inspection
of a table of statistics of values from century to century,
that the value of money fell about four-fifths towards the
end of the sixteenth century, while other commodities preserved practically the same relative values, would consider
it very probable that an absolute change had taken place
in the value of money, even if he were ignorant of the

discovery of mines in America. On the other hand, if he
should see the price of wheat double from one year to the
next without any remarkable variation in the price of most
other articles or in their relative values, he would attribute
it to an absolute change in the value of wheat, even if he
did not know that a bad grain harvest had preceded the
high price.

Without reference to this extreme case, where the disturb-
ance of the system of relative values is explained by the
movement of a single article, it is evident that among all
the possible hypotheses on absolute variations some explain
the relative variations more simply and more probably than
others.

If, without being limited to consideration of the system
of relative values at two distinct periods, observation follows
it through its intermediate states, a new set of data will be
provided to determine the most probable law of absolute
variations, from all possibilities for satisfying the observed
law of relative variations.

9. Let

$$p_1, \ p_2, \ p_3, \ \text{etc.,}$$

be the values of certain articles, with reference to a gram of
silver ; if the standard of value is changed and a myriagram
of wheat is substituted for the gram of silver, the values of
the same articles will be given by the expressions

$$\frac{1}{a} p_1, \ \frac{1}{a} p_2, \ \frac{1}{a} p_3, \ \text{etc.,}$$

a being the price of the myriagram of wheat, or its value
with reference to a gram of silver.   In general, whenever it

is desired to change the standard of value, it will suffice to multiply the numerical expressions of individual values by a constant factor, greater or less than unity ; just as with a system of points conditioned to remain in a straight line, it would suffice to know the distances from these points to any one of their number, to determine by the addition of a constant number, positive or negative, their distances referred to another point of the system, taken as the new origin.

From this there results a very simple method of expressing by a mathematical illustration the variations which occur in the relative values of a system of articles. It is sufficient to conceive of a system composed of as many points arranged in a straight line as there are articles to be compared, so that the distances from one of these points to all the others constantly remain proportional to the logarithms of the numbers which measure the values of all these articles with reference to one of their number. All the changes of distance which occur by means of addition and subtraction, from the relative and absolute motions of such a system of movable points, will correspond perfectly to the changes by means of multiplication and division in the system of values which is being compared : from which it follows that the calculations for determining the most probable hypothesis as to the absolute movements of a system of points, can be applied, by going from logarithms back to numbers, to the determination of the most probable hypothesis for the absolute variations of a system of values.

But, in general, such calculations of probability, in view of the absolute ignorance in which we would be of the causes of variation of values, would be of very slight interest.

What is really important is to know the laws which govern the variation of values, or, in other words, the theory of wealth. This theory alone can make it possible to prove to what absolute variations are due the relative variations which come into the field of observation; in the same manner (if it is permissible to compare the most exact of sciences with the one nearest its cradle) as the theory of the laws of motion, begun by Galileo and completed by Newton, alone makes it possible to prove to what real and absolute motions are due the relative and apparent motions of the solar system.

10. To sum up, there are only relative values; to seek for others is to fall into a contradiction with the very idea of *value in exchange*, which necessarily implies the idea of a ratio between two terms. But also an accomplished change in this ratio is a relative effect, which can and should be explained by absolute changes in the terms of the ratio. There are no absolute values, but there are movements of absolute rise and fall in values.

Among the possible hypotheses on the absolute changes which produce the observed relative changes, there are some which the general laws of probability indicate as most probable. Only knowledge of the special laws of the matter in question can lead to the substitution of an assured decision for an opinion as to probability.

11. If theory should indicate one article incapable of absolute variation in its value, and should refer to it all others, it would be possible to immediately deduce their absolute variations from their relative variations; but very slight attention is sufficient to prove that such a fixed term

does not exist, although certain articles approach much more nearly than others to the necessary conditions for the existence of such a term.

The monetary metals are among the things which, under ordinary circumstances and provided that too long a period is not considered, only experience slight absolute variations in their value. If it were not so, all transactions would be disturbed, as they are by paper money subject to sudden depreciation.*

On the other hand, articles such as wheat, which form the basis of the food supply, are subject to violent disturbances ; but, if a sufficient period is considered, these disturbances balance each other, and the average value approaches fixed conditions, perhaps even more closely than the monetary metals. This will not make it impossible for the value so determined to vary, nor prevent it from actually experiencing absolute variations on a still greater scale of time. Here, as in astronomy, it is necessary to recognize *secular* variations, which are independent of *periodic* variations.

Even the wages of that lowest grade of labour, which is only considered as a kind of mechanical agent, the element often proposed as the standard˜ of value, is subject like wheat to periodic as well as secular variations ; and, if the periodic oscillations of this element have generally been less

* What characterizes a contract of sale, and distinguishes it essentially from a contract of exchange, is the invariability of the absolute value of the monetary metals, at least for the lapse of time covered by an ordinary business transaction. In a country where the absolute value of the monetary tokens is perceptibly variable, there are, properly speaking, no contracts of sale. This distinction should affect some legal questions.

wide than those of wheat, on the other hand we may sus-
pect that in future the progressive changes in the social
status will cause it to suffer much more rapid secular
variations.

But if no article exists having the necessary conditions for
perfect fixity, we can and ought to imagine one, which, to
be sure, will only have an abstract existence.*   It will
only appear as an auxiliary term of comparison to facilitate
conception of the theory, and will disappear in the final
applications.

In like manner, astronomers imagine a mean sun endowed
with a uniform motion, and to this imaginary star they refer,
as well the real sun as the other heavenly bodies, and so
finally determine the actual situation of these stars with
reference to the real sun.

12. It would perhaps seem proper to first investigate the
causes which produce absolute variations in the value of
the monetary metals, and, when these are accounted for, to
reduce to the corrected value of money the variations which
occur in the value of other articles. *This corrected money*
would be the equivalent of the mean sun of astronomers.

But, on one hand, one of the most delicate points in the
theory of wealth is just this analysis of the causes of variation of the value of the monetary metals used as means of
circulation, and on the other hand it is legitimate to admit,
as has been already said, that the monetary metals do not
suffer notable variations in their values except as we compare very distant periods, or else in case of sudden revolu-
tions, now very improbable, which would be caused by the

* Montesquieu, *Esprit des Lois*, Book XXII, Chap. 8.

discovery of new metallurgical processes, or of new mineral deposits. It is, to be sure, a common saying, that the price of money is steadily diminishing, and fast enough for the depreciation of value of coin to be very perceptible in the course of a generation; but by going back to the cause of this phenomenon, as we have shown how to do in this chapter, it is plain that the relative change is chiefly due to an absolute upward movement of the prices of most of the articles which go directly for the needs or pleasures of mankind, an ascending movement produced by the increase in population and by the progressive developments of industry and labour. Sufficient explanations on this doctrinal point can be found in the writings of most modern economists.

Finally, in what follows, it will be the more legitimate to neglect the absolute variations which affect the value of the monetary metals, as we do not have numerical applications directly in view. If the theory were sufficiently developed, and the data sufficiently accurate, it would be easy to go from the value of an article in terms of a fictitious and invariable modulus, to its monetary value. If the value of an article, in terms of this fictitious modulus, was p, at a time when that of the monetary metal was π, and if at another time these quantities had taken other values, p' and π', it is evident that the monetary value of the article would have varied in the ratio of

$$\frac{p}{\pi} \text{ to } \frac{p'}{\pi'}.$$

If the absolute value of the monetary metals during long periods only suffers slow variations, which are hardly perceptible throughout the commercial world, the relative values of these very metals suffer slight variations from one commercial centre to another, which constitute what is known as the *rate of exchange*, and of which the mathematical formula is very simple, as will be seen in the next chapter.

CHAPTER III

OF THE EXCHANGES

13. The time will doubtless come when all civilized peoples will appreciate the benefit of uniformity of measures. One of the titles of the French Revolution to the gratitude of future generations, is that it initiated this great social improvement; and, in spite of national and political prejudices, this example has not lacked imitators.

The uniformity and stability of measures acquire a still greater importance when we have to do with the monetary system, so often turned upside down by the selfishness and bad faith of governments. Moreover, the state of society in the different countries of Europe makes impossible the return to the disorder in which so simple a thing in itself as the monetary system remained for so long a time and among almost all peoples. It would be superfluous to repeat observations on this subject, which have become perfectly familiar.

Let us suppose then that all commercial peoples have adopted the same monetary unit, for instance, one gram of fine silver, or, what amounts to the same thing, that the ratio of each monetary unit to a gram of fine silver be permanently established. Knowledge of these ratios forms a large part of what is known among those engaged in the

business as the science of exchange. This science, which
can be summed up in a table found everywhere, should not
distract our attention. In other words, we have nothing to
do with nominal exchange, but only with actual exchange,
i.e. the ratio between the values in exchange of the same
weight of fine silver according as it is payable in different
places. It is plain also that the cost of exchange, or the difference of the ratio of exchange from unity, cannot exceed
the cost of transportation of this weight of fine silver from
one place to the other, when free trade in the precious
metals is allowed between the two places, or the cost of
transportation plus the expense of smuggling when this
trade is embarrassed by prohibitory laws. To find the
equations of exchange, we will suppose, to begin with, that
the cost of exchange is less than the cost of transportation,
or that the exchange takes place without any real transportation of money, without any change in the distribution
of the precious metals between the two commercial centres.

14. Let us suppose at first only two centres of exchange. Let us designate by $m_{1,2}$ the total of the sums
for which the centre (1) is annually indebted to the centre
(2); and by $m_{2,1}$ the total of the sums for which the place
(2) is annually indebted to the place (1); by $c_{1,2}$ the rate
of exchange at the place (1) on the place (2), or the
amount of silver given at the place (2) in exchange for a
weight of silver expressed by 1 and payable at the place
(1).

Adopting this notation, and starting from the hypothesis
that the two places balance their account without transport-
ing money in either direction, it is plain that we shall have

$$m_{1,2}c_{1,2} = m_{2,1}, \text{ or } c_{1,2} = \frac{m_{2,1}}{m_{1,2}}.$$

We have in general $c_{2,1} = \dfrac{1}{c_{1,2}}$,

and in this particular case $c_{2,1} = \dfrac{m_{1,2}}{m_{2,1}}$.

Whenever, therefore, the ratio $\dfrac{m_{2,1}}{m_{1,2}}$ only differs from unity by a quantity less than the cost of transportation of a monetary unit from one place to the other, the balance between the two places will be settled without actual transportation of money and by the mere effect of the rate of exchange.

Let us now suppose any number of places in correspondence, and let $m_{i,k}$ express generally the total of the sums annually due from the place (i) to the place (k), and $c_{i,k}$ the coefficient of exchange from (i) to (k). The number of these coefficients for a number of places (r) will be $r(r-1)$; but, as in general, $c_{i,k} = \dfrac{1}{c_{k,i}}$, the number of coefficients to be determined is reduced at the outset to $\dfrac{r(r-1)}{2}$.

Nor are all these coefficients mutually independent; for if, for instance,

$$c_{i,k} > c_{i,l} \times c_{l,k},$$

any one having to convey money from (k) to (i), instead of getting a draft from (k) on (i), will find it cheaper to get one from (k) on (l) which he can exchange for one from (l) on (i). For the same reason it is impossible to have

$$c_{i,k} < c_{i,l} \times c_{l,k},$$

for this is equivalent to

$$c_{i,l} > \frac{c_{i,k}}{c_{l,k}}$$

or $\qquad\qquad c_{i,l} > c_{i,k} \times c_{k,l},$

which has just been proved impossible, whatever the letters i, k, l may be.

Thus we have in general

(a) $\qquad\qquad c_{i,k} = c_{i,l} \times c_{l,k},$

or at least, if this relation temporarily ceases to be satisfied, banking transactions continually tend to reëstablish it. But our analysis only considers that state of equilibrium about which commercial changes cause the rates of exchange to oscillate continually.

The relation (a) can be represented geometrically by imagining a series of points (i), (k), (l), ... so placed that the distance between each two points, such as (i), (k) is measured by the logarithm of the number $c_{i,k}$. By means of this convention the relation (a) expresses that the points (i), (k), (l), and in general all the points of the series, equal in number to the centres of exchange, must be situated in the same straight line.

From this it results that it is enough to know the coefficients of exchange from one centre to all the others, to deduce the rates for all the centres from one to the other. On this account there only remains a number of unknown coefficients expressed by $r - 1$, r being the number of the centres of exchange.

15. Now it is easy to find as many equations as there are centres in correspondence, starting always from the hypothe-

sis that there is no actual transportation of money from
one centre to another, and that thus what one centre owes
to all the others is, at this first centre, of precisely the same
value as what all the others owe to it.

From this consideration the following equations are obtained :

$$(b) \begin{cases} m_{1,2} + m_{1,3} + \cdots + m_{1,r} = m_{2,1}c_{2,1} + m_{3,1}c_{3,1} + \cdots \\ \qquad\qquad\qquad\qquad\qquad + m_{r,1}c_{r,1}, \\ m_{2,1} + m_{2,3} + \cdots + m_{2,r} = m_{1,2}c_{1,2} + m_{3,2}c_{3,2} + \cdots \\ \qquad\qquad\qquad\qquad\qquad + m_{r,2}c_{r,2}, \\ m_{3,1} + m_{3,2} + \cdots + m_{3,r} = m_{1,3}c_{1,3} + m_{2,3}c_{2,3} + \cdots \\ \qquad\qquad\qquad\qquad\qquad + m_{r,3}c_{r,3}, \\ \cdots\cdots\cdots\cdots\cdots\cdots\cdots \\ m_{r,1} + m_{r,2} + \cdots + m_{r,r-1} = m_{1,r}c_{1,r} + m_{2,r}c_{2,r} + \cdots \\ \qquad\qquad\qquad\qquad\qquad + m_{r-1,r}c_{r-1,r}. \end{cases}$$

These equations are in number r, while, by what has just
been said, all the unknown coefficients can be expressed in
functions of the coefficients $c_{1,2}$, $c_{1,3}$, $\cdots c_{1,r}$, which are only
$r-1$ in number. It must therefore be that one of the
above equations is involved in the others; and, in fact, if
we put

$$(c) \begin{cases} c_{1,2} = \dfrac{1}{c_{2,1}}, \; c_{1,3} = \dfrac{1}{c_{3,1}}, \cdots c_{1,r} = \dfrac{1}{c_{r,1}}, \\ c_{3,2} = c_{3,1} \times c_{1,2} = \dfrac{c_{3,1}}{c_{2,1}}, \\ \cdots\cdots\cdots\cdots\cdots \\ c_{r-1,r} = \dfrac{c_{r-1,1}}{c_{r,1}}, \end{cases}$$

D

the equations (*b*) become:

$$(d)\begin{cases} m_{1,2} + m_{1,3} + \cdots + m_{1,r} = m_{2,1}c_{2,1} + m_{3,1}c_{3,1} + \cdots \\ \qquad\qquad\qquad\qquad\qquad\qquad + m_{r,1}c_{r,1}, \\ (m_{2,1} + m'_{2,3} + \cdots + m'_{2,r})c_{2,1} = m_{1,2} + m'_{3,2}c_{3,1} + \cdots \\ \qquad\qquad\qquad\qquad\qquad\qquad + m'_{r,2}c_{r,1}, \\ (m_{3,1} + m\ddot{}_{3,2} + \cdots + m_{3,r})c_{3,1} = m_{1,3} + m'_{2,3}c_{2,1} + \cdots \\ \qquad\qquad\qquad\qquad\qquad\qquad + m'_{r,3}c_{r,1}, \\ \cdot\ \cdot\ \cdot\ \cdot\ \cdot\ \cdot\ \cdot\ \cdot\ \cdot\ \cdot\ \cdot\ \cdot\ \cdot\ \cdot\ \cdot\ \cdot \\ (m_{r,1} + m\check{}_{r,2} + \cdots + m_{r,r-1})c_{r,1} = m_{1,r} + m'_{2,r}c_{2,1} + \cdots \\ \qquad\qquad\qquad\qquad\qquad\qquad + m_{r\ 1,r}c_{r-1,1}. \end{cases}$$

Adding all these equations together except the first, and eliminating from each member the terms which cancel, we obtain again the first equation. Thus there are only just as many distinct equations as there are independent variables.

Where only three centres are considered, the equations (*d*) would become

$$m_{1,2} + m_{1,3} = m_{2,1}c_{2,1} + m_{3,1}c_{3,1},$$

$$(m_{2,1} + m_{2,3})c_{2,1} = m_{1,2} + m_{3,2}c_{3,1},$$

$$(m_{3,1} + m_{3,2})c_{3,1} = m_{1,3} + m_{2,3}c_{2,1}.$$

From this can be obtained:

$$c_{2,1} = \frac{m_{3,1}m_{1,2} + m_{1,2}m_{3,2} + m_{1,3}m_{3,2}}{m_{2,1}m_{3,1} + m_{2,1}m_{3,2} + m_{3,1}m_{2,3}},$$

$$c_{3,1} = \frac{m_{2,1}m_{1,3} + m_{1,2}m_{2,3} + m_{1,3}m_{2,3}}{m_{2,1}m_{3,1} + m_{2,1}m_{3,2} + m_{3,1}m_{2,3}},$$

and consequently

$$c_{3,2} = \frac{m_{2,1}m_{1,3} + m_{1,2}m_{2,3} + m_{1,3}m_{2,3}}{m_{3,1}m_{1,2} + m_{1,2}m_{3,2} + m_{1,3}m_{3,2}}.$$

The composition of the values of $c_{2,1}$, $c_{3,1}$, and $c_{3,2}$, in this particular case, shows clearly enough how the ratio of $m_{1,2}$ to $m_{2,1}$ can vary considerably, without causing great variations in the value of $c_{2,1}$; or, in other words, how the interconnection of centres of exchange diminishes the variations in the rate of exchange from one place to another.

16. The preceding analysis assumes that the value of each coefficient, such as $c_{2,1}$, does not fall below a certain limit $\gamma_{2,1}$, which depends on the cost of actual transportation of the monetary unit from the centre (2) to the centre (1), including the premium for smuggling if the laws interfere with exportation of the precious metals. Thus if $p_{2,1}$ indicates this cost of transportation, the superior limit of $c_{1,2}$ will be

$$1 + p_{2,1},$$

and for the inferior limit of $c_{2,1}$ we shall have

$$\gamma_{2,1} = \frac{1}{1 + p_{2,1}}.$$

If on the other hand the equations (c) and (d) give

$$c_{2,1} < \gamma_{2,1},$$

it will be concluded that the hypothesis which excludes actual transportation of money from the centre (2) to the centre (1) is inadmissible, and that consequently the two first equations (d),

$$m_{1,2} + m_{1,3} + \cdots + m_{1,r} = m_{2,1}c_{2,1} + m_{3,1}c_{3,1} + \cdots + m_{r,1}c_{r,1},$$

$$(m_{2,1} + m_{2,3} + \cdots + m_{2,r})c_{2,1} = m_{1,2} + m_{3,2}c_{3,1} + \cdots + m_{r,2}c_{r,1},$$

cease to hold true, since they express that the centres (1) and (2) balance their debits and credits by the compensa-

tion of exchange alone, without either exportation or importation of money. It will be necessary to replace the
unknown quantity $c_{2,1}$ by the constant $\gamma_{2,1}$ in the other
equations (d) ; and as these equations number $r - 2$, they
will be just enough to determine the $r - 2$ remaining
unknown quantities, *i.e.* $c_{3,1}$, $c_{4,1} \cdots c_{r,1}$.

Reverting to the meaning of the first two equations of
(b), which cease to be true under the present hypothesis,
it is evident that the net sum imported at the centre (1),
after deducting the cost of transportation, will be

$$I = m_{2,1}\gamma_{2,1} + m_{3,1}c_{3,1} + \cdots$$
$$+ m_{r,1}c_{r,1} - (m_{1,2} + m_{1,3} + \cdots + m_{1,r}),$$

and that the sum exported from the centre (2), including
the cost of transportation, is expressed by

$$E = m_{2,1} + m_{2,3} + \cdots$$
$$+ m_{2,r} - (m_{1,2}\gamma_{1,2} + m_{3,2}c_{3,2} + \cdots + m_{r,2}c_{r,2}).$$

Furthermore, we will have

(e) $E\gamma_{2,1} = I,$

since the difference between E and I arises only from the
cost of transportation from (2) to (1). This equation of
condition must therefore reduce to an identity by means of
the values of $c_{3,1}, \ldots c_{r,1}$, derived from the equations (d)
after substituting for $c_{2,1}$ its real value of $\gamma_{2,1}$. If, now, we
add the equations (d) except the first two, which are no
longer true in this case, and if we cross out the terms which
cancel, we shall come to an equation of condition precisely
identical with equation (e).

17. It is noteworthy that the relation

(a) $$c_{i,k} = c_{i,l} \times c_{l,k}$$

continues to hold even when the coefficients c attain their limits γ in consequence of actual transportation of specie from one place to the other. The former argument for this equation is as applicable to the present case. If we have, for instance,

$$\gamma_{i,k} > \gamma_{i,l} \times c_{l,k},$$

any one wishing to send funds from (k) to (i), instead of paying the actual cost of this transportation, would get a draft at (k) on (l), and with the proceeds of the draft would have specie shipped from (l) to (i). If, on the other hand,

$$\gamma_{i,k} < \gamma_{i,l} \times c_{l,k},$$

the deduction would be

$$\gamma_{i,l} > \gamma_{i,k} \times c_{k,l},$$

and any one having funds to send from (l) to (i) would get a draft at (l) on (k) and ship the proceeds to (i). In consequence, even if we suppose the ratio

$$\gamma_{i,k} = \gamma_{i,l} \times c_{l,k}$$

to be temporarily disturbed, banking operations constantly tend to reëstablish it.

A singular consequence of this, and nevertheless a very strict one, at least in theory, is, that if three banking centres are considered, (i), (k), and (l), there will always be at least two between which there will be no direct shipments

of specie, or between which exchange will be effected by
simple shifting of values, without actual transportation of
money and without the rate of exchange touching the limit
which it would reach if the rate were fixed by the actual
cost of transportation from one of these centres to the other.
In fact, if there could be an actual transportation of specie
from (i) to (k), from (i) to (l), and from (k) to (l), as the
causes which fix the cost of actual transportation from (i) to·
(k) are independent of those which fix the cost between (i)
and (l), and as neither depend in any way on those which
fix the price between (k) and (l), it would be infinitely
improbable, or physically impossible, that the coefficients $\gamma_{i,k}$,
$\gamma_{i,l}$ and $\gamma_{l,k}$ should exactly satisfy the equation of condition

$$\gamma_{i,k} = \gamma_{i,l} \times \gamma_{l,k}.$$

It is easy to see that this principle is not one of rigorous
application in practice, for the rate of exchange is not fixed
with mathematical accuracy, and there may be also special
reasons for coin shipments when the cost of transportation
does not too far exceed the loss in buying exchange.   In
this question, as in all which arise under the theory of
wealth, the principles deduced from theory are of general
applicability, but must not be rigorously applied to each
individual case.

18.   What has just been said of three centres of exchange
is equally true of any number of centres.   If this number
is designated by r, the number of coefficients of exchange
will be $r(r-1)$, but by virtue of the equations (c) it is
enough to know $r-1$ of these coefficients to determine
all the others.   Supposing, then, that $r-1$ coefficients,

such as $c_{i,k}$ reach their [lower] limiting values as $\gamma_{i,k}$, because there is an actual movement of specie between the centres, as between (i) and (k); the inverse coefficients, such as $c_{k,i}$ will also reach their [upper] limiting values; but there will be $r(r-1) - 2(r-1) = (r-1)(r-2)$ coefficients, such as $c_{k,l}$, which will not reach their limiting values; so that the equalization of credits between the centres (k) and (l) will take place by banking transfers, without actual transportation of coin.

In other words, by the present hypothesis, all the centres which form a part of the system will import or export money, but there will not be import or export between every pair of centres. Of the total number of combinations $\dfrac{r(r-1)}{2}$ between the centres, there will be $r-1$ which will correspond to actual transportation of specie, and $\dfrac{(r-1)(r-2)}{2}$ which will correspond to simple banking transfers.

Moreover, this must necessarily be so; for otherwise the amounts which must flow annually from one place to the other would be indeterminate; which cannot be accepted as true. And, in fact, if we extend to any number of places the reasoning which we have employed above to determine the amount imported and exported when there is actual transportation of specie between two places only, it will be recognized that, to determine the total of each import or export, there cannot be more than r equations, which are easily deduced from the equations (b) or (d), and which even reduce to $r-1$ distinct equations. The number of quantities to be determined, therefore, is also reduced to $r-1$, and consequently there can only be between the centres $r-1$ combinations which correspond to real movements of specie.

But if it could be admitted that for a particular case

$$\gamma_{i, k} = \gamma_{i, l} \times \gamma_{l, k},$$

as this equation would mean that it costs exactly as much to transport a sum of money from (k) to (i) as to send it first from (k) to (l) and then from (l) to (i), there would then be no method, according to the data, to determine completely what would be the sums transported from one of these places to the other, and also, in this case, there would be more unknown quantities than equations. It is evident, therefore, that all the results of this analysis are intimately connected.

19. All commercial nations employ simultaneously gold and silver as monetary metals,* and hence arise certain relations between the course of exchange and the comparative prices of gold and silver in different commercial centres. As before, let us call $c_{i, k}$ the coefficient of exchange from

* The Russian government has struck some platinum coins; but, as Babbage very well observes in his book on manufacturing industry, platinum so far lacks one of the essential qualities of a money metal: an ingot of platinum is worth much more in a single mass then when cut up, on account of the difficulty and expense of all processes for obtaining platinum in large masses. As foreign coins have only the value of the precious metal contained in them, it follows that in foreign parts platinum money would be worth much less than the ingots used in making it. For a like reason subsidiary coinage is worth less in foreign parts than the silver contained in it was worth in ingots, on account of the expense necessary for purifying the metal for conversion into ingots. Consequently any government would be unwise to make subsidiary coinage beyond the requirements for small change in its own jurisdiction.

the centre (i) to the centre (k), or the amount of silver given at (k) in exchange for a weight of silver expressed by 1, and payable at (i) ; let us also designate by ρ_i the ratio of the price of gold to the price of silver at (i), or the number of grams of silver given at (i) for one gram of gold, and by ρ_k the ratio of the price of gold to the price of silver at (k). Let us also suppose that if an amount h in gold coin is transported from (i) to (k), this sum will be reduced to $\epsilon_{i,k} h$, after subtracting the cost of actual transportation and the cost of smuggling, in case prohibitory laws embarrass the export of gold from (i) to (k).

With a weight of gold expressed by h, a weight of silver can be bought at (i) expressed by $\rho_i h$, and payable at the same place ; with this same weight of silver, or with the equivalent weight of gold, a weight of silver can be bought expressed by $\rho_i c_{i,k} h$, and payable at (k). But the weight of gold expressed by h, if it were actually transported to the centre (k), would be reduced to $\epsilon_{i,k} h$, after subtracting the cost of transportation, and would buy at this latter place a weight of silver expressed by $\rho_k \epsilon_{i,k} h$; hence actual transportation will take place if we have

$$\rho_k \epsilon_{i,k} h > \rho_i c_{i,k} h, \text{ or } \frac{\rho_k}{\rho_i} > \frac{c_{i,k}}{\epsilon_{i,k}}.$$

As long as this inequality holds, there will be a flow of gold from (i) to (k) ; as gold becomes scarcer at (i), it will be more sought after ; the ratio of the value of gold to silver will rise at (i), and, for the same reason, this ratio will fall at (k) until we reach

$$\frac{\rho_k}{\rho_i} = \text{ or } < \frac{c_{i,k}}{\epsilon_{i,k}}.$$

Repetition of the same argument, or mere permutation of the subscript letters, shows that after equilibrium is established we must have

$$\frac{\rho_i}{\rho_k} = \text{ or } < \frac{c_{k,i}}{\epsilon_{k,i}};$$

that is to say,

$$\frac{\rho_k}{\rho_i} = \text{ or } > c_{i,k} \times \epsilon_{k,i},$$

on account of the ratio

$$c_{k,i} = \frac{1}{c_{i,k}};$$

moreover, the determination of the number $\epsilon_{k,i}$ follows by permutation of subscripts from that of the number $\epsilon_{i,k}$.

The more the values $\epsilon_{i,k}$, $\epsilon_{k,i}$ approach to unity, the narrower the limits between which is restricted the value of the coefficient $c_{i,k}$, when the ratio $\frac{\rho_k}{\rho_i}$ is given, or reciprocally the value of the ratio $\frac{\rho_k}{\rho_i}$, when the coefficient of exchange $c_{i,k}$ is given. If these numbers differ only slightly from unity, as will ordinarily be the case, on account of the ease of exporting gold at slight expense, and of eluding, if necessary, prohibitory laws, we shall practically have $\frac{\rho_k}{\rho_i} = c_{i,k}$.

In this case the price of gold at one centre and the coefficients of exchange are data enough to deduce the value of gold at all the other centres with which the first has banking relations. It is vain for governments in instituting their monetary system to fix a legal ratio for the value of gold and that of silver (as in France, where the law assigns to this ratio the value 15.5) ; if the value of gold, resulting from the conditions given above, is greater, gold will command a premium with dealers in exchange, and will thus recover its true commercial value.

No change would be caused in the foregoing argument by the supposition that the coefficient of exchange $c_{i, k}$ reaches its limiting value, which value has been termed previously $\gamma_{i, k}$.

The cost of coinage and the seigniorage which most governments charge for the making of coin raises the price of a gram of silver or a gram of gold coined above the price of a gram of silver or gold uncoined or in ingots throughout the national domain.

This added value disappears whenever the coin goes abroad, where it is only valued for its fineness and weight ; it is as if the cost of transportation were increased by the amount of this loss which exportation causes for the money of any nation, and by this means it can be considered without modifying the preceding analysis.

Coinage gives to copper pieces a value far above the intrinsic value of the metal. For this reason copper pieces are not exported, and constitute a conventional coinage which only circulates in its national domain.

The wear of coin, or the loss of weight which coins suffer by long use, is another consideration which influences banking operations. For these technical details the works may be consulted of those authors who have gone into the question in detail, and particularly the treatise of Smith.

CHAPTER IV

OF THE LAW OF DEMAND

20. To lay the foundations of the theory of exchangeable values, we shall not accompany most speculative writers back to the cradle of the human race ; we shall undertake to explain neither the origin of property nor that of exchange or division of labour. All this doubtless belongs to the history of mankind, but it has no influence on a theory which could only become applicable at a very advanced state of civilization, at a period when (to use the language of mathematicians) the influence of the *initial* conditions is entirely gone.

We shall invoke but a single axiom, or, if you prefer, make but a single hypothesis, *i.e.* that each one seeks to derive the greatest possible value from his goods or his labour. But to deduce the rational consequences of this principle, we shall endeavour to establish better than has been the case the elements of the data which observation alone can furnish. Unfortunately, this fundamental point is one which theorists, almost with one accord, have presented to us, we will not say falsely, but in a manner which is really meaningless.

It has been said almost unanimously that " the price of goods is in the inverse ratio of the quantity offered, and in the direct ratio of the quantity demanded." It has never been considered that the statistics necessary for accurate numerical estimation might be lacking, whether of the quantity offered or of the quantity demanded, and that this might prevent deducing from this principle general consequences capable of useful application. But wherein does the principle itself consist? Does it mean that in case a double quantity of any article is offered for sale, the price will fall one-half? Then it should be more simply expressed, and it should only be said that the price is in the inverse ratio of the quantity offered. But the principle thus made intelligible would be false ; for, in general, that 100 units of an article have been sold at 20 francs is no reason that 200 units would sell at 10 francs in the same lapse of time and under the same circumstances. Sometimes less would be marketed ; often much more.

Furthermore, what is meant by the quantity demanded? Undoubtedly it is not that which is actually marketed at the demand of buyers, for then the generally absurd consequence would result from the pretended principle, that the more of an article is marketed the dearer it is. If by demand only a vague desire of possession of the article is understood, without reference to the *limited price* which every buyer supposes in his demand, there is scarcely an article for which the demand cannot be considered indefinite ; but if the price is to be considered at which each buyer is willing to buy, and the price at which each seller is willing to sell, what becomes of the pretended principle? It is not, we repeat, an erroneous proposition — it is a proposition devoid of meaning. Consequently all those

who have united to proclaim it have likewise united to make
no use of it.   Let us try to adhere to less sterile principles.

The cheaper an article is, the greater ordinarily is the
demand for it.   The sales or the demand (for to us these
, two words are synonymous, and we do not see for what
reason theory need take account of any demand which
does not result in a sale) — the sales or the demand generally, we say, increases when the price decreases.

We add the word *generally* as a corrective; there are, in
fact, some objects of whim and luxury which are only
desirable on account of their rarity and of the high price
which is the consequence thereof.   If any one should suc-
ceed in carrying out cheaply the crystallization of carbon,
and in producing for one franc the diamond which to-day
is worth a thousand, it would not be astonishing if diamonds
should cease to be used in sets of jewellery, and should disappear as articles of commerce.   In this case a great fall in
price would almost annihilate the demand.   But objects of this
nature play so unimportant a part in social economy that it is
not necessary to bear in mind the restriction of which we speak.

The demand might be in the inverse ratio of the price;
ordinarily it increases or decreases in much more rapid
proportion — an observation especially applicable to most
manufactured products.   On the contrary, at other times
the variation of the demand is less rapid; which appears
(a very singular thing) to be equally applicable both to the
most necessary things and to the most superfluous.   The
price of violins or of astronomical telescopes might fall one-
half and yet probably the demand would not double; for
this demand is fixed by the number of those who cultivate

the art or science to which these instruments belong ; who have the disposition requisite and the leisure to cultivate them and the means to pay teachers and to meet the other necessary expenses, in consequence of which the price of the instruments is only a secondary question. On the contrary, firewood, which is one of the most useful articles, could probably double in price, from the progress of clearing land or increase in population, long before the annual consumption of fuel would be halved ; as a large number of consumers are disposed to cut down other expenses rather than get along without firewood.

21. Let us admit therefore that the sales or the annual demand D is, for each article, a particular function $F(p)$ of the price p of such article. To know the form of this function would be to know what we call *the law of demand* or *of sales*. It depends evidently on the kind of utility of the article, on the nature of the services it can render or the enjoyments it can procure, on the habits and customs of the people, on the average wealth, and on the scale on which wealth is distributed.

Since so many moral causes capable of neither enumeration nor measurement affect the law of demand, it is plain that we should no more expect this law to be expressible by an algebraic formula than the law of mortality, and all the laws whose determination enters into the field of statistics, or what is called social arithmetic. Observation must therefore be depended on for furnishing the means of drawing up between proper limits a table of the corresponding values of D and p ; after which, by the well-known methods of interpolation or by graphic processes, an empiric formula or a curve can be made to represent the function in question ; and the solution of problems can be pushed as far as numerical applications.

But even if this object were unattainable (on account of the difficulty of obtaining observations of sufficient number and accuracy, and also on account of the progressive variations which the law of demand must undergo in a country which has not yet reached a practically stationary condition), it would be nevertheless not improper to introduce the un-known law of demand into analytical combinations, by means of an indeterminate symbol ; for it is well known that one of the most important functions of analysis consists precisely in assigning determinate relations between quantities to which numerical values and even algebraic forms are abso-lutely unassignable.

Unknown functions may none the less possess properties or general characteristics which are known ; as, for instance, to be indefinitely increasing or decreasing, or periodical, or only real between certain limits. Nevertheless such data, however imperfect they may seem, by reason of their very generality and by means of analytical symbols, may lead up to relations equally general which would have been difficult to discover without this help. Thus without know-ing the law of decrease of the capillary forces, and starting solely from the principle that these forces are inappreciable at appreciable distances, mathematicians have demonstrated the general laws of the phenomena of capillarity, and these laws have been confirmed by observation.

On the other hand, by showing what determinate rela-tions exist between unknown quantities, analysis reduces these unknown quantities to the smallest possible number, and guides the observer to the best observations for discovering their values.   It reduces and coördinates statistical documents ; and it diminishes the labour of statisticians at the same time that it throws light on them.

For instance, it is impossible *a priori* to assign an algebraic form to the law of mortality ; it is equally impossible to formulate the function expressing the subdivision of population by ages in a stationary population ; but these two functions are connected by so simple a relation, that, as soon as statistics have permitted the construction of a table of mortality, it will be possible, without recourse to new observations, to deduce from this table one expressing the proportion of the various ages in the midst of a stationary population, or even of a population for which the annual excess of deaths over births is known.*

Who doubts that in the field of social economy there is a mass of figures thus mutually connected by assignable relations, by means of which the easiest to determine empirically might be chosen, so as to deduce all the others from it by means of theory?

22. We will assume that the function $F(p)$, which expresses the law of demand or of the market, is a *continuous* function, *i.e.* a function which does not pass suddenly from one value to another, but which takes in passing all inter-

---

* The *Annuaire du Bureau des Longitudes* contains these two tables, the second deduced from the first, as above, and calculated on the hypothesis of a stationary population.

The work by Duvillard, entitled *De l'influence de la petite vérole sur la mortalité*, contains many good examples of mathematical connections between essentially empirical functions.

E

mediate values.   It might be otherwise if the number of
consumers were very limited : thus in a certain household
the same quantity of firewood will possibly be used whether
wood costs 10 francs or 15 francs the stere,* and the
consumption may suddenly be diminished if the price
of the stere rises above the latter figure.   But the wider
the market extends, and the more the combinations of
needs, of fortunes, or even of caprices, are varied among
consumers, the closer the function $F(p)$ will come to vary-
ing with p in a continuous manner.   However little may be
the variation of p, there will be some consumers so placed
that the slight rise or fall of the article will affect their consumptions, and will lead them to deprive themselves in some
way or to reduce their manufacturing output, or to substitute
something else for the article that has grown dearer, as, for
instance, coal for wood or anthracite for soft coal.   Thus the
" exchange " is a thermometer which shows by very slight
variations of rates the fleeting variations in the estimate
of the chances which affect government bonds, variations
which are not a sufficient motive for buying or selling to
most of those who have their fortunes invested in such bonds.

If the function $F(p)$ is continuous, it will have the property common to all functions of this nature, and on which
so many important applications of mathematical analysis are
based : *the variations of the demand will be sensibly proportional to the variations in price so long as these last are
small fractions of the original price.*   Moreover, these variations will be of opposite signs, *i.e.* an increase in price will
correspond with a diminution of the demand.

[* 1 stere = 1 M^8 = 35.3 cu. ft. = ᴀ cord. — TRANSLATOR.]

Suppose that in a country like France the consumption of sugar is 100 million kilograms when the price is 2 francs a kilogram, and that it has been observed to drop to 99 millions when the price reached 2 francs 10 centimes. Without considerable error, the consumption which would correspond to a price of 2 francs 20 centimes can be valued at 98 millions, and the consumption corresponding to a price of 1 franc 90 centimes at 101 millions. It is plain how much this principle, which is only the mathematical consequence of the continuity of functions, can facilitate applications of theory, either by simplifying analytical expressions of the laws which govern the movement of values, or in reducing the number of data to be borrowed from experience, if the theory becomes sufficiently developed to lend itself to numerical determinations.

Let us not forget that, strictly speaking, the principle just enunciated admits of exceptions, because a continuous function may have interruptions of continuity in some points of its course ; but just as friction wears down roughnesses and softens outlines, so the wear of commerce tends to suppress these exceptional cases, at the same time that commercial machinery moderates variations in prices and tends to maintain them between limits which facilitate the application of theory.

23. To define with accuracy the quantity D, or the function $F(p)$ which is the expression of it, we have supposed that D represented the quantity sold *annually* throughout the extent of the country or of the market * under consider-

* It is well known that by *market* economists mean, not a certain place where purchases and sales are carried on, but the entire territory of which

ation. In fact, the year is the natural unit of time, especially for researches having any connection with social
economy. All the wants of mankind are reproduced
during this term, and all the resources which mankind
obtains from nature and by labour. Nevertheless, the price
of an article may vary notably in the course of a year, and,
strictly speaking, the law of demand may also vary in the
same interval, if the country experiences a movement of
progress or decadence. For greater accuracy, therefore, in
the expression $F(p)$, p must be held to denote the annual
average price, and the curve which represents function F to
be in itself an average of all the curves which would represent this function at different times of the year. But this
extreme accuracy is only necessary in case it is proposed to
go on to numerical applications, and it is superfluous for
researches which only seek to obtain a general expression
of average results, independent of periodical oscillations.

24. Since the function $F(p)$ is continuous, the function
$pF(p)$, which expresses the total value of the quantity
annually sold, must be continuous also. This function would
equal zero if p equals zero, since the consumption of any
article remains finite even on the hypothesis that it is absolutely free ; or, in other words, it is theoretically always
possible to assign to the symbol p a value so small that the
product $pF(p)$ will vary imperceptibly from zero. The
function $pF(p)$ disappears also when p becomes infinite, or,
in other words, theoretically a value can always be assigned
to p so great that the demand for the article and the pro-

the parts are so united by the relations of unrestricted commerce that prices
there take the same level throughout, with ease and rapidity.

duction of it would cease. Since the function $pF(p)$ at first increases, and then decreases as p increases, there is therefore a value of p which makes this function a maximum, and which is given by the equation,

$$(1) \qquad F(p) + pF'(p) = 0;$$

in which F', according to Lagrange's notation, denotes the differential coefficient of function F.

If we lay out the curve anb (Fig. 1), of which the abscissas oq and the ordinates qn represent the variables p and D, the root of equation (1) will be the abscissa of the point n from which the triangle ont, formed by the tangent nt and the radius vector on, is isosceles, so that we have $oq = qt$.

We may admit that it is impossible to determine the function $F(p)$ empirically for each article, but it is by no means the case that the same obstacles prevent the approximate determination of the value of p which satisfies equation (1) or which renders the product $pF(p)$ a maximum. The construction of a table, where these values could be found, would be the work best calculated for preparing for the practical and rigorous solution of questions relating to the theory of wealth.

But even if it were impossible to obtain from statistics the value of p which should render the product $pF(p)$ a maximum, it would be easy to learn, at least for all articles to which the attempt has been made to extend commercial statistics, whether current prices are above or below this value. Suppose that when the price becomes $p + \Delta p$, the annual consumption as shown by statistics, such as custom-house records, becomes $D - \Delta D$. According as

$$\frac{\Delta D}{\Delta p} < \text{ or } > \frac{D}{p},$$

the increase in price, Δp, will increase or diminish the product $pF(p)$; and, consequently, it will be known whether the two values p and $p + \Delta p$ (assuming Δp to be a small fraction of p) fall above or below the value which makes the product under consideration a maximum.

Commercial statistics should therefore be required to separate articles of high economic importance into two categories, according as their current prices are above or below the value which makes a maximum of $pF(p)$. We shall see that many economic problems have different solutions, according as the article in question belongs to one or the other of these two categories.

25. We know by the theory of maxima and minima that equation (1) is satisfied as well by the values of p which render $pF(p)$ a minimum as by those which render this product a maximum. The argument used at the beginning of the preceding article shows, indeed, that the function $pF(p)$ necessarily has a maximum, but it might have several and pass through minimum values between. A root of equation (1) corresponds to a maximum or a minimum according as

$$2\, F'(p) + pF''(p) < \text{ or } > 0,$$

or, substituting for p its value and considering the essentially negative sign of $F'(p)$,

$$2\, [F'(p)]^2 - F(p) \times F''(p) > \text{ or } < 0.$$

In consequence, whenever $F''(p)$ is negative, or when the

curve $D = F(p)$ turns its concave side to the axis of the abscissas, it is impossible that there should be a minimum, nor more than one maximum. In the contrary case, the existence of several maxima or minima is not proved to be impossible.

But if we cease considering the question from an exclu sively abstract standpoint, it will be instantly recognized how improbable it is that the function $pF(p)$ should pass through several intermediate maxima and minima inside of the limits between which the value of p can vary; and as it is unnecessary to consider maxima which fall beyond these limits, if any such exist, all problems are the same as if the function $pF(p)$ only admitted a single maximum. The essential question is always whether, for the extent of the limits of oscillation of p, the function $pF(p)$ is increasing or decreasing for increasing values of p.

Any demonstration ought to proceed from the simple to the complex : the simplest hypothesis for the purpose of investigating by what laws prices are fixed, is that of monopoly, taking this word in its most absolute meaning, which supposes that the production of an article is in one man's hands. This hypothesis is not purely fictitious : it is realized in certain cases ; and, moreover, when we have studied it, we can analyze more accurately the effects of competition of producers.

CHAPTER V

OF MONOPOLY

26. For convenience in discussion, suppose that a man finds himself proprietor of a mineral spring which has just been found to possess salutary properties possessed by no other. He could doubtless fix the price of a *liter* of this water at 100 francs; but he would soon see by the scant demand, that this is not the way to make the most of his property. He will therefore successively reduce the price of the liter to the point which will give him the greatest possible profit; *i.e.* if $F(p)$ denotes the law of demand, he will end, after various trials, by adopting the value of p which renders the product $pF(p)$ a maximum, or which is determined by the equation

$$(1) \qquad F(p) + pF'(p) = 0.$$

The product $\qquad pF(p) = \dfrac{[F(p)]^2}{-F'(p)}$

will be the annual revenue of the owner of the spring, and this revenue will only depend on the nature of function F.

To make equation (1) applicable, it must be supposed that for the value of p obtained from it, there will be a corresponding value of D which the owner of the spring can deliver, or which does not exceed the annual flow of

this spring ; otherwise the owner could not, without damage
to himself, reduce the price per liter as low as would be for
his interest were the spring more abundant. If the spring
produces annually a number of liters expressed by Δ, by
deducing p from the relation $F(p) = \Delta$, we necessarily obtain
the price per liter which must finally be fixed by the competition of customers.

27. In this simplest case, chosen for a type, the producer has no cost of production to bear, or the cost can
be considered insignificant. Let us go on to that of a
man who possesses the secret of a medical preparation or
an artificial mineral water, for which the materials and labour
must be paid for. .It will no longer be the function $pF(p)$,
or the annual *gross receipts*, which the producer should strive
to carry to its maximum value, but the *net receipts*, or the
function $pF(p) - \phi(D)$, in which $\phi(D)$ denotes the cost of
making a number of liters equal to D. Since D is connected with p by the relation $D = F(p)$, the complex function
$pF(p) - \phi(D)$ can be regarded as depending implicitly
on the single variable p, although generally the cost of production is an explicit function, not of the price of the article produced, but of the quantity produced. Consequently
the price to which the producer should bring his article will
be determined by the equation

$$(2) \qquad D + \frac{dD}{dp}\left[p - \frac{d[\phi(D)]}{dD}\right] = 0.$$

This price will fix in turn the annual net receipts or the
revenue of the inventor, and the capital value of his secret,
or his *productive property*, the ownership of which is guar-

anteed by law and can have commercial circulation as well as that of a piece of land or any material property. If this value is nil or insignificant, the owner of the property will obtain no pecuniary profit from it ; he will abandon it gratis, or for a very small payment, to the first comer who seeks to develop it. The value of a liter will only represent the value of the raw materials, the wages or profits of the agents who coöperate in making and marketing it, and the interest on the capital necessary for development.

28. The terms of our example prevent our admitting in this case a limitation of the productive forces, which would hinder the producer from lowering the price to the rate which would give the *maximum* net receipts, according to the law of demand.   But in a great many other cases there may be such a limitation, and if Δ expresses the limit which the production or the demand cannot exceed, the price will be fixed by the relation $F(p) = \Delta$, as if there were no cost of production.   The cost, in this case, is not borne by the consumers at all ; it only diminishes the income of the producer. It falls not exactly on the proprietor (who, unless the inventor or first holder, — a question of original conditions with which theory has nothing to do, — acquired the property, himself or through his agents, for a value proportioned to its revenue), but on the property itself. A decrease of this cost will only be to the advantage of the producer, so far as it does not result in the possibility of increasing his producing power.

29. Let us return to the case where this possibility exists, and where the price p is determined according to equation (2). We shall observe that the coefficient $\dfrac{d[\phi(D)]}{dD}$,

though it may increase or decrease as D increases, must be supposed to be positive, for it would be absurd that the *absolute* expense of production should decrease as production increases. We shall call attention also to the fact that necessarily $p > \dfrac{d[\phi(D)]}{dD}$, for dD being the increase of production, $d[\phi(D)]$ is the increase in the cost, pdD is the increase of the gross receipts, and whatever may be the abundance of the source of production, the producer will always stop when the increase in expense exceeds the increase in receipts. This is also abundantly evident from the form of equation (2), since D is always a positive quantity, and $\dfrac{dD}{dp}$ a negative quantity.

In the course of our investigations we shall seldom have occasion to consider $\phi(D)$ directly, but only its differential coefficient $\dfrac{d[\phi(D)]}{dD}$, which we will denote by $\phi'(D)$. This differential coefficient is a new function of D, the form of which exerts very great influence on the principal problems of economic science.

The function $\phi'(D)$ is capable of increasing or decreasing as D increases, according to the nature of the producing forces and of the articles produced.

For what are properly called *manufactured articles*, it is generally the case that the cost becomes proportionally less as production increases, or, in other words, when D increases $\phi'(D)$ is a decreasing function. This comes from better organization of the work, from discounts on the price of raw materials for large purchases, and finally from the reduction of what is known to producers as *general expense*.

It may happen, however, even in exploiting products of this nature, that when the exploitation is carried beyond certain limits, it induces higher prices for raw materials and labour, to the point where $\phi'(D)$ again begins to increase with D.

Whenever it is a question of working agricultural lands, of mines, or of quarries, *i.e.* of what is essentially real estate, the function $\phi'(D)$ increases with D; and, as we shall soon see, it is in consequence of this fact alone that farms, mines, and quarries yield a net revenue to their owners, long before all has been extracted from the soil which it is physically able to produce, and notwithstanding the great subdivision of these properties, which causes between producers a competition which can be considered as unlimited. On the contrary, investments made under the condition that as D increases $\phi'(D)$ decreases, can only yield a net income or a *rent* in the case of a monopoly properly so-called, or of a competition sufficiently limited to allow the effects of a monopoly collectively maintained to be still perceptible.

30. Between the two cases where the function $\phi'(D)$ is increasing and decreasing, there falls naturally the one where this function reduces to a constant, the cost being constantly proportional to the production, and where equation (2) takes the form

$$D + \frac{dD}{dp}(p - g) = 0.$$

The case must also be pointed out where $\phi(D)$ is a constant, and $\phi'(D) = 0$, so that the price is the same as if there were no cost. This case occurs more frequently than would be suspected at first glance, especially where we have to do with production under a monopoly, and where the value of the number D receives the extension of which it admits. For instance, in a theatrical enterprise D denotes the number of tickets sold, and the cost of the enterprise remains practically the same, without reference to the number of spectators. For the tolls of a bridge, which is another monopolistic investment, D denotes the number of passengers ; and the costs for repairs, watching, and bookkeeping will be the same, whether the crossing is much or little used. In such cases the constant g disappears, equation (2) becomes the same as equation (1), and the price p is determined in the same manner as if there were no costs.

31. It seems a matter of course that when the cost of production increases, the price fixed by the monopolist, according to equation (2), will increase likewise ; but, on consideration, it will appear that so important a proposition should be supported by a rational demonstration ; and furthermore, this demonstration will lead us to an equally important observation, which only mathematics can incontestably establish.

Let p_0 be the root of equation (2) which we will put in the form

$$(3) \qquad F(p) + F'(p)[p - \psi(p)] = 0,$$

as $\phi'(D) = \phi'[F(p)]$ can be more simply replaced by $\psi(p)$; and suppose that, as the function $\psi(p)$ varies by a quantity u, and becomes $\psi(p) + u$, p becomes $p_0 + \delta$. If we neglect the squares and higher powers of the increments u and δ, equation (3) will establish the following relation between these two increments :

(4) $\{F'(p_0)[2 - \psi'(p_0)] + F''(p_0)[p_0 - \psi(p_0)]\}\delta$
            $- uF'(p_0) = 0 ;$

the coefficient of δ in this expression being the derivative with respect to p of the first member of equation (3), in which derivative the value p_0 has been given to p.

But this coefficient of δ is necessarily negative, according to the well-known theory of maxima and minima ; for if it were positive, the root p_0 of equation (3) would correspond to the minimum of the function $pF(p) - \phi(D)$, and not to the maximum of this function, as it should. Moreover $F'(p)$ is by its nature a negative quantity. In general, therefore, the increment δ is of the same sign as the increment u.

32. This result has been demonstrated on the supposition that the variations u, δ are very small quantities, of which the squares and products can be neglected without sensible error, but by a very simple argument this restriction can be removed. In fact, whatever the increase of cost denoted by u, it can be supposed that the function $\psi(p)$ passes from the value $\psi(p)$ to the value $\psi(p) + u$ by a series of very small increments, u_1, u_2, u_3, etc., all of the same sign. At the same time p will pass from the value p_0 to the value $p_0 + \delta$ by a series of corresponding increments, also very small, δ_1, δ_2, δ_3, etc. ; δ_1 will be (according to the preceding paragraph) of the same sign as u_1, δ_2 as u_2, etc. Therefore,

$$\delta = \delta_1 + \delta_2 + \delta_3 + \text{etc.,}$$

will be of the same sign as

$$u = u_1 + u_2 + u_3 + \text{etc.}$$

This method of demonstration should be borne in mind, as it will be frequently recurred to.

33. From equation (4) we obtain

$$\frac{\delta}{u} = \frac{F'(p_0)}{F'(p_0)[2 - \psi'(p_0)] + F''(p_0)[p_0 - \psi(p_0)]},$$

and since both terms of the fraction in the second member are negative, we conclude that δ will be numerically greater or less than u according as we have

$$- F'(p_0) \gtrless - F'(p_0)[2 - \psi'(p_0)] - F''(p_0)[p_0 - \psi(p_0)],$$

or, in other words,

$$F'(p_0)[1 - \psi'(p_0)] + F''(p_0)[p_0 - \psi(p_0)] \gtrless 0,$$

which, by replacing $p_0 - \psi(p_0)$ by its value as deduced from equation (3), becomes

$$[F'(p_0)]^2[1 - \psi'(p_0)] - F(p_0) \times F''(p_0) \lessgtr 0.$$

34. To make this more obvious by numerical applications, let us take a fictitious case. Suppose that the function $\phi'(D)$ were at first $= 0$, and that it subsequently reduces to a constant g. The first value of p or p_0 will be given by the equation

$$F(p) + pF'(p) = 0;$$

the second value of p, which we will call p', will be given by another equation

$$(5) \qquad F(p) + (p - g)F'(p) = 0.$$

Suppose, in the first place, that $F(p) = \dfrac{a}{b + p}$; the values of p_0 and p', according to the preceding equations, will be respectively

$$p_0 = \sqrt{b}, \text{ and } p' = g + \sqrt{b + g^2} = g + \sqrt{p_0^2 + g^2}$$

(the root of equation (5) which would give a negative value for p' must necessarily be excluded). In this case we see that p' is greater than p_0 by a quantity greater than g, *i.e.* greater than the amount of the new cost imposed on the production. If, for instance, the new cost is one-tenth of the original price, or if $g = \frac{1}{10} p_0$, we shall have $p' = p_0\, 1.1488$; the increase in price will be very nearly one and one-half tenths; the old price being 20 francs and the cost 2 francs, the new price will be 23 francs, or, more exactly, 22 francs 97 centimes.*

Suppose, in the second place, $F(p) = \dfrac{a}{b + p^3}$, we shall have $p_0 = \sqrt[3]{\dfrac{b}{2}}$; and equation (5) will become

$$2p^3 - 3gp^2 - b = 0,$$

or $\qquad\qquad p^3 - \tfrac{3}{2}gp^2 - p_0^3 = 0,$

which by the ordinary method of solution will give

$$p' = \tfrac{1}{2}\left\{ g + \sqrt[3]{g^3 + 4p_0^3 + 2\sqrt{2p_0^3(g^3 + 2p_0^3)}} \right.$$
$$\left. + \sqrt[3]{g^3 + 4p_0^3 - 2\sqrt{2p_0^3(g^3 + 2p_0^3)}} \right\}.$$

In this case the excess of p' over p_0 will be less than g.

---

* NOTE BY THE TRANSLATOR. — The figures given above are as they appear in the original French, but there was evidently a mistake in arithmetic made by the author, who used under the radical $p_0^2 + g$ instead of $p_0^2 + g^2$. The figures should be $p' = p_0 \times 1.1050$, and the new price 22 francs and 10 centimes.

If $g = \frac{1}{10}p_0$, we shall have $p' = p_0 \times 1.0505$. Thus if the new cost is one-tenth of the original price, the increase in price will only be one-half of one-tenth of that price. The old price being 20 francs, and the added cost 2 francs, the new price will be only 21 francs, or, more exactly, 21 francs .01 centime.

35. The result which we have just reached is well worth attention : it shows us that, according to the form of the function $F(p)$, or according to the law of demand, an increase in the cost of production augments the price of a commodity, for which there exists a monopoly, sometimes much more and sometimes much less than the increase in cost ; and that, in the same manner, there is no equality between the reduction of cost and fall in the price of the commodity.

It results from this, that if the new cost were not met by the producer himself, but by the consumer, or by an intermediate agent, who would be reimbursed by the consumer, this increase in cost, which would always make the article dearer for the consumer, and which would always diminish the net income of the producer, might, according to circumstances, produce an advance or a decline in the price paid to the producer.

Reciprocally, a fall in the cost of *transmission*, or in that of passing the commodity from the possession of the producer to that of the consumer, may have the effect at one time of increasing the price paid to the producer, and at another time of diminishing it ; but in all cases it will diminish the final price paid by the consumer, and will cause an increase in the net income of the producer.

F

All those expenses which are incurred with a view to preparing for final consumption the crude commodity as it leaves the producers' hands, must in this respect be considered in the same light as costs of transmission.

However, this calculation is only applicable in the case where the producer can meet the demand which gives him the greatest net return, and reduce his price as much as is necessary to attain this maximum return. In other cases, he will produce all he can, before as well as after the change in the cost, whether of production or of transmission, and the cost price to the consumer will remain invariable, because in a condition of equilibrium, and on a large scale, there cannot be two different prices for the same quantity marketed. The increase of cost, therefore, from whatever source, must finally be wholly borne by the producer.

CHAPTER VI

OF THE INFLUENCE OF TAXATION ON COMMODITIES PRODUCED
UNDER A MONOPOLY

36. The considerations developed at the close of the preceding chapter are of course applicable to the theory of taxation. The burden of taxation makes what might be called an artificial cost, adjusted according to a more or less systematic plan, and of which at least the distribution, if not the general rate, is within the power of the legislator to determine; and consequently the theory of the incidence of taxation is one of the great objects of investigations in Political Economy.

The forms of taxation may vary widely. At the time when public affairs were conducted in secret, it was considered a great art to be able so to diversify forms as, it was thought, to increase the supplies to the treasury without making its exactions felt. Later, according to a half-understood theory, it was considered desirable to make taxation as uniform as possible; but the financial legislation which stands to-day in France is equally removed from both these extremes and recognizes forms of taxation essentially distinct, though quite limited in number, which, from practical rather than theoretical considerations, it classes in two main categories of direct and indirect taxes. The levy assessed according to the assumed net income of a land-owner or of a producer is a direct tax. The excise which must be paid on an article before it reaches the consumer's hands is an indirect tax; and we intend to consider only these two kinds of taxation. It should be borne in mind, that in this chapter only those articles are considered of which the production is controlled by a monopoly.

If a tax, either fixed or proportional to his net income, is laid upon a monopolist producer, it is plain, according to explanations in the two preceding chapters, that this tax will have no direct influence on the price of the article which he produces, and consequently none on the quantity produced, and that it will not be a burden to the consumer in any way. Its only immediate result is to diminish the income and the capitalized wealth of the producer.

It can even be said that this tax only injures first holders, inventors, and, in general, those who were profiting by the property at the time when the tax was laid, and such of their successors as have obtained the property gratuitously. For successors who have to pay regulate their purchase price according to the net returns, after deduction of the tax. If the capitalized value is reduced while the property is in their hands, it is a real disaster for them.

Even though this tax does not affect consumers it may be nevertheless very prejudicial to public interests, not principally because, by reducing the wealth of the producer so taxed, it reduces his means as a consumer and affects the law of demand for other articles; but especially because the part withdrawn by the tax from the income of the producer is ordinarily employed in a manner less advantageous for the increase of the annual product, the national wealth, and the comfort of the people, than if it had remained at the disposal of the producer himself. We will not consider here the effects on the distribution of the products of nature and of labour of such a levy, although this is undoubtedly the final object of all problems connected with the theory of wealth.

But it is possible to say, in agreement with all authorities, that even though it does not prevent invested capital from producing as much as before its taxation, a tax on the income of the producer is an obstacle to the creation of new investments and even to the improvement of existing ones, if a proportional tax is to be considered. No one will embark his capital in new investments, nor in the improvement of existing investments, if he can no longer obtain the ordinary interest brought in by capital in enterprises of the same kind, on account of the tax imposed on the net income from his investment. It is by closing an avenue of employment for labour and industry, that such a tax, when exaggerated, has its most disastrous effect.

Bounties, an invention of modern times, are the opposite of taxes. To use an algebraic expression, they are a negative tax, so that the same analytical formulas are applicable to taxation and bounties. But bounties differ from taxes in being reckoned on the gross product; it has never been proposed to grant a bounty on the net product, so that it is only for the sake of system that we mention bounties at all here in connection with taxation on income or net product.

37. The tax may and generally does consist in a fixed

charge levied on each unit of a commodity, or one of which the product is proportional to D. Its effects are the same as if the function $\phi'(D)$ were increased by a constant i. An increase in cost to the consumer must always result from it, and a decrease of consumption or production; but, according to circumstances, the increase of cost to the consumer may be greater or less than i. It makes no difference in the absolute effects of taxation to producer or consumers, from whom the tax is collected, or at what period the revenue collector reaches the commodity; only the apparent effects will vary according as the producer does or does not pay the tax in advance; *i.e.* if he advances it, the price of the commodity as it leaves his hands will always be increased by taxation; in the opposite case this price may rise in some cases and fall in others.

However, in saying that the absolute effects of taxation are the same, whether the producer does or does not pay the tax in advance, we mean to restrict this proposition to the case in which only the principal is considered, and where the additional charges arising from interest on this principal are neglected. When the commodity must pass through many hands before reaching consumers, as each intermediate agent must employ additional capital, if the article has already paid its tribute, so evidently the commodity will be sold at a higher price to consumers just in proportion as the tax is prematurely collected; and the consumption will be further reduced correspondingly. It is important, therefore, to consumers, to producers, and even to the treasury, that the tax should be paid late, and, if possible, by the consumer himself; although, on the other hand, the collection of a tax becomes more expensive by subdivisions, and tends more to excite complaints by the masses, *i.e.* the consumers, because it makes the operation of the revenue department more evident to them.

38. Let us call p_0 the price of the commodity before the tax, and p' the price which follows imposition of the tax. p_0 will be the root of the equation

$$F(p) + [p - \psi(p)]F'(p) = 0 ;$$

and p' that of the equation

$$F(p) + [p - \psi(p) - i]F'(p) = 0.$$

With an approximation proportionally greater as i becomes smaller relatively to p_0, we shall have

$$p' - p_0 = \frac{i[F'(p_0)]^2}{[F'(p_0)]^2[2 - \psi'(p_0)] - F(p_0)F''(p_0)}.$$

The pecuniary loss borne by consumers, who continue to buy the commodity notwithstanding the increased price, will be

$$(p' - p_0)F(p') ;$$

the *gross* profit of the treasury will be

$$iF(p') ;$$

so that the loss of consumers alone will exceed this gross profit in all cases where we have

$$p' - p_0 > i ;$$

i.e. in the same cases where imposition of the tax would increase the price on leaving the producer's hands when he does not pay the tax in advance.

The loss of net income borne by the monopolist will be

$$p_0F(p_0) - \phi[F(p_0)] - \{p'F(p') - \phi[F(p')] - iF(p')\}$$
$$= p_0F(p_0) - \phi[F(p_0)] - \{p'F(p') - \phi[F(p')]\} + iF(p').$$

But, since p_0 is the value of p which renders the function

$$pF(p) - \phi[F(p)]$$

a maximum, we must necessarily have

$$p_0F(p_0) - \phi[F(p_0)] > p'F(p') - \phi[F(p')],$$

and therefore the loss to the monopolist alone will exceed the gross profit of the treasury. The loss borne by consumers will therefore remain without any compensation, and there is no doubt that the doctrine of Quesnay's school is perfectly applicable to the products of monopoly ; namely, that it is better to levy a direct tax on the net income of the monopolist than to lay a specific tax on the commodity.

The amount spent in consumption of the article before the tax was $p_0F(p_0)$; after the tax it becomes $p'F(p')$ and we must necessarily have

$$p_0F(p_0) > p'F(p').$$

This results from the inequality just proved

$$p_0F(p_0) - \phi[F(p_0)] > p'F(p') - \phi[F(p')]$$

and from this other inequality

$$\phi[F(p_0)] > \phi[F(p')],$$

which is self-evident, since the absolute amount of the cost of production cannot change except by decreasing when the quantity produced decreases.

The value of i, or the rate of tax, which will make the gross profit of the treasury a maximum, can be obtained from the following equation :

$$\frac{d[iF(p')]}{di} = F(p') + iF'(p')\frac{dp'}{di} = 0,$$

and p' is furthermore a function of i which is given by the equation

$$F(p') + [p' - \psi(p') - i]F'(p') = 0.$$

39. If the law of demand and the productive property are such that the producer, whether before or after imposition of the tax, is unable to supply the demand which would produce the greatest profit, he will sell all his product, as well after as before imposition of the tax, and will sell it at the same price, because, in a stable condition of things, there cannot be two prices corresponding to the same output. The tax will therefore fall entirely on the producer.

From this it seems as if, in fixing the amount of this tax, the treasury would only be limited by the condition of not entirely absorbing the net income of the producer. But this consequence would be inexact, and the error can be proved at least in one case ; namely, that where $\phi'(D)$ increases with D, and where we have at the same time $p' - p_0 > i$, p_0 and p' being respectively the roots of the equations

(1) $$F(p) + [p - \phi'(D)]F'(p) = 0,$$

and $$F(p) + [p - \phi'(D) - i]F'(p) = 0.$$

In fact, if Δ is the necessary limit of production, and π the value of p derived from the relation $F(p) = \Delta$, it would be necessary for the hypothesis that $\pi > p'$, and *a fortiori*

$\pi > p_0 + i$, i being equal to $\pi - \dfrac{\phi(\Delta)}{\Delta}$. We should therefore have

$$\pi > p_0 + \pi - \frac{\phi(\Delta)}{\Delta}, \text{ or } p_0 < \frac{\phi(\Delta)}{\Delta}.$$

But this last inequality certainly cannot hold true if $\phi'(D)$ is (according to the hypothesis) a function which increases with D; for then, p_0 being smaller than π, the demand D_0 corresponding to p_0 is greater than Δ, and $\dfrac{\phi(D_0)}{D_0}$ is greater than $\dfrac{\phi(\Delta)}{\Delta}$; p_0 would therefore be less than $\dfrac{\phi(D_0)}{D_0}$. This value of p_0 would therefore cause a loss to the producer and consequently could not be the root of equation (1).

40. If the government, instead of imposing a tax, grants a bounty i to the producer under a monopoly, the price, which was p_0 before the bounty, will fall, and will become p'. According to circumstances, we shall have $p_0 - p' \gtrless i$. The loss to the public treasury will be $iF(p')$; the gain to such consumers as were buying before the bounty will be $(p_0 - p')F(p_0)$, and will have no necessary relation to $iF(p')$. As for the consumers who only buy after the fall in price resulting from the bounty, it is impossible to assert that the premium has benefited them pecuniarily; it has only diverted their money from one line of use to apply it to the line thus favoured.

The change in the net income of the producer which occurs as a consequence of the bounty is :

$$p'F(p') - \phi[F(p')] + iF(p') - [p_0F(p_0) - \phi[F(p_0)]]$$
$$= iF(p') - \{p_0F(p_0) - \phi[F(p_0)] - [p'F(p') - \phi[F(p')]]\}.$$

But, since p_0 is the value of p which renders a maximum the function

$$pF(p) - \phi[F(p)],$$

it always follows that

$$p_0F(p_0) - \phi[F(p_0)] > p'F(p') - \phi[F(p')],$$

so that the gain resulting from the premium to the producer (and in general it is the interest of the producer, and not that of the consumers, which is considered in establishing a bounty) is essentially less than the public sacrifice at the cost of which this gain is attained.

41. Taxation may be imposed according to a rate not specific but proportional to the selling price; in other words, the tax, instead of being expressed by the constant i, is expressed by the term np.* In this case, if the commodity were produced and delivered without appreciable cost between producer and consumers, the price being determined by the condition that the producer shall derive the greatest possible profit, or that $(1 - n)pF(p)$ shall be a maximum, the presence of the constant factor $(1 - n)$ will not alter the value of p in the least; the tax will fall wholly on the producer, and might go so far as to absorb all his net income.

In the opposite case, the only one which can ordinarily be realized, the condition would be that the function

$$(1 - n)pF(p) - \phi(D)$$

* There is a portion of the cost which may be considered to act as such a tax, *i.e.* as being proportional to the cost of the commodity. This is the portion which pays the interest on the capital employed in marketing the commodity.

should attain a maximum, or that we should have

$$(2) \quad F(p) + \left\{ p - \frac{1}{1-n} \phi'[F(p)] \right\} F'(p) = 0;$$

so that imposition of the tax would have absolutely the same effects as if all the items of cost requisite for the production of the commodity and its distribution to the consumers were increased in the proportion of $1 \div \dfrac{1}{1-n}$; a very simple result, and one which merits attention.

Thus a tax of this nature, circumstances being otherwise unchanged, will be the heavier the higher the costs of production and distribution already are, or the smaller the proportion of the price of the commodity represented by the profit of the monopolist.

The gross profit of the treasury is $np'F(p')$. The value of n which makes it a maximum is given by the equation

$$\frac{d[np'F(p')]}{dn} = 0,$$

or
$$p'F(p') + \frac{dp'}{dn} n [F(p') + p'F'(p')] = 0.$$

The loss borne by consumers who continue to buy the commodity will be $(p' - p_0)F(p')$; so that this loss will be greater or less than the gross profit to the treasury according as $p' - p_0 \gtrless np'$, or as $p'(1-n) \gtrless p_0$.

The loss borne by the producer will be

$$p_0 F(p_0) - \phi[F(p_0)] - \{(1-n)p'F(p') - \phi[F(p')]\}$$
$$= p_0 F(p_0) - \phi[F(p_0)] - \{p'F(p') - \phi[F(p')]\} + np'F(p').$$

This loss alone will therefore exceed the gross profit of the treasury, as in the other kind of taxation.

42. There remains for discussion the effect of taxation *in kind* on the price of an article under a monopoly. We will take this up only very briefly, as this form of taxation everywhere tends to disappear, owing to the industrial development of nations. We will distinguish here two different cases.

It is possible that the product of a tax in kind may be applied to a consumption which would not take place if it were not for the tax, and to one which has no influence on the demand which other consumers make on the producer. Let us first suppose the amount paid in kind equal to a constant K. The equation for the maximum, from which the value of p is to be deduced, instead of

$$F(p) + \{p - \phi'[F(p)]\}F'(p) = 0,$$

will become

$$(3) \quad F(p) + \{p - \phi'[F(p) + K]\}F'(p) = 0,$$

so that such a tax will raise or lower the price of the article, according as the function $\phi'(D)$ increases or decreases for increasing values of D.

Let us next suppose the amount paid in kind to be proportional to the gross production, and to be in the ratio of $n + 1$ to this gross production. The function which it is the producer's interest to render a maximum will be

$$pF(p) - \phi\left[\frac{F(p)}{1 - n}\right],$$

and equation (3) will be replaced by

$$F(p) + \left\{ p - \frac{1}{(1-n)} \phi'\left[\frac{F(p)}{1-n}\right]\right\} F'(p) = 0.$$

If, on the other hand, the law of the consumption of the commodity is supposed to remain the same before as after the taxation in kind, we shall have for the function which must be a maximum in case of a fixed payment K,

$$p[F(p) - K] - \phi[F(p)],$$

and for its differential which determines the value of p,

$$F(p) - K + \{p - \phi'[F(p)]\} F'(p) = 0.$$

An exaction proportional to the gross product, or a *tithe*, would give for the function for the maximum

$$(1 - n)pF(p) - \phi[F(p)],$$

of which the differential would be the same as the first member of equation (2). Thus the price of the commodity, the profit to the treasury, the burden on consumers, and the loss to the producer would be absolutely the same as if the commodity had had imposed on it a tax proportional to the price in the ratio of $n \div 1$.

CHAPTER VII

OF THE COMPETITION OF PRODUCERS

43. Every one has a vague idea of the effects of competition. Theory should have attempted to render this idea more precise; and yet, for lack of regarding the question from the proper point of view, and for want of recourse to symbols (of which the use in this connection becomes indispensable), economic writers have not in the least improved on popular notions in this respect. These notions have remained as ill-defined and ill-applied in their works, as in popular language.

To make the abstract idea of monopoly comprehensible, we imagined one spring and one proprietor. Let us now imagine two proprietors and two springs of which the qualities are identical, and which, on account of their similar positions, supply the same market in competition. In this case the price is necessarily the same for each proprietor. If p is this price, $D = F(p)$ the total sales, D_1 the sales from the spring (1) and D_2 the sales from the spring (2), then $D_1 + D_2 = D$. If, to begin with, we neglect the cost of production, the respective incomes of the proprietors will be pD_1 and pD_2; and *each of them independently* will seek to make this income as large as possible.

We say *each independently*, and this restriction is very

essential, as will soon appear ; for if they should come to an agreement so as to obtain for each the greatest possible income, the results would be entirely different, and would not differ, so far as consumers are concerned, from those obtained in treating of a monopoly.

Instead of adopting $D = F(p)$ as before, in this case it will be convenient to adopt the inverse notation $p = f(D)$; and then the profits of proprietors (1) and (2) will be respectively expressed by

$$D_1 \times f(D_1 + D_2), \text{ and } D_2 \times f(D_1 + D_2),$$

i.e. by functions into each of which enter two variables, D_1 and D_2.

Proprietor (1) can have no direct influence on the determination of D_2 : all that he can do, when D_2 has been determined by proprietor (2), is to choose for D_1 the value which is best for him. This he will be able to accomplish by properly adjusting his price, except as proprietor (2), who, seeing himself forced to accept this price and this value of D_1, may adopt a new value for D_2, more favourable to his interests than the preceding one.

Analytically this is equivalent to saying that D_1 will be determined in terms of D_2 by the condition

$$\frac{d[D_1 f(D_1 + D_2)]}{dD_1} = 0,$$

and that D_2 will be determined in terms of D_1 by the analogous condition

$$\frac{d[D_2 f(D_1 + D_2)]}{dD_2} = 0,$$

whence it follows that the final values of D_1 and D_2, and consequently of D and of p, will be determined by the system of equations

(1) $\qquad f(D_1 + D_2) + D_1 f'(D_1 + D_2) = 0,$

(2) $\qquad f(D_1 + D_2) + D_2 f'(D_1 + D_2) = 0.$

Let us suppose the curve $m_1 n_1$ (Fig. 2) to be the plot of equation (1), and the curve $m_2 n_2$ that of equation (2), the variables D_1 and D_2 being represented by rectangular coordinates. If proprietor (1) should adopt for D_1 a value represented by ox_1, proprietor (2) would adopt for D_2 the value oy_1, which, for the supposed value of D_1, would give him the greatest profit. But then, for the same reason, producer (1) ought to adopt for D_1 the value ox_{11}, which gives the maximum profit when D_2 has the value oy_1. This would bring producer (2) to the value oy_{11} for D_2, and so forth ; from which it is evident that an equilibrium can only be established where the coördinates ox and oy of the point of intersection i represent the values of D_1 and D_2. The same construction repeated on a point of the figure on the other side of the point i leads to symmetrical results.

The state of equilibrium corresponding to the system of values ox and oy is therefore *stable;* i.e. if either of the producers, misled as to his true interest, leaves it temporarily, he will be brought back to it by a series of reactions, constantly declining in amplitude, and of which the dotted lines of the figure give a representation by their arrangement in steps.

The preceding construction assumes that $om_1 > om_2$ and $on_1 < on_2$: the results would be diametrically opposite if

G

these inequalities should change sign, and if the curv
m_1n_1 and m_2n_2 should assume the disposition represente
by Fig. 3. The coördinates of the point *i*, where the tw
curves intersect, would then cease to correspond to a stat
of stable equilibrium. But it is easy to prove that such
disposition of the curves is inadmissible. In fact, if $D_1 = c$
equations (1) and (2) reduce, the first to

$$f(D_2) = 0,$$

and the second to

$$f(D_2) + D_2f'(D_2) = 0.$$

The value of D_2 derived from the first would correspond
to $p = 0$; the value of D_2 derived from the second corresponds to a value of p which would make the product pD_2 a
maximum. Therefore the first root is necessarily greater
than the second, or $om_1 > om_2$, and for the same reason
$on_2 > on_1$.

44. From equations (1) and (2) we derive first $D_1 = D_2$
(which ought to be the case, as the springs are supposed to
be similar and similarly situated), and then by addition :

$$2f(D) + Df'(D) = 0,$$

an equation which can be transformed into

$$(3) \qquad D + 2p\frac{dD}{dp} = 0,$$

whereas, if the two springs had belonged to the same property, or if the two proprietors *had come to an understanding*, the value of p would have been determined by the
equation

$$(4) \qquad D + p\frac{dD}{dp} = 0,$$

and would have rendered the total income Dp a *maximum*, and consequently would have assigned to each of the producers a greater income than what they can obtain with the value of p derived from equation (3).

Why is it then that, for want of an understanding, the producers do not stop, as in the case of a monopoly or of an association, at the value of p derived from equation (4), which would really give them the greatest income?

The reason is that, producer (1) having fixed his production at what it should be according to equation (4) and the condition $D_1 = D_2$, the other will be able to fix his own production at a higher or lower rate with a *temporary benefit.* To be sure, he will soon be punished for his mistake, because he will force the first producer to adopt a new scale of production which will react unfavourably on producer (2) himself. But these successive reactions, far from bringing both producers nearer to the original condition [of monopoly], will separate them further and further from it. In other words, this condition is not one of stable equilibrium ; and, although the most favourable for both producers, it can only be maintained by means of a formal engagement ; for in the moral sphere men cannot be supposed to be free from error and lack of forethought any more than in the physical world bodies can be considered perfectly rigid, or supports perfectly solid, etc.

45. The root of equation (3) is graphically determined by the intersection of the line $y = 2x$ with the curve $y = -\dfrac{F(x)}{F'(x)}$; while that of equation (4) is graphically shown by the intersection of the same curve with the line $y = x$.

But, if it is possible to assign a real and positive value to the function $y = - \dfrac{F(x)}{F'(x)}$ for every real and positive value of x, then the abscissa x of the first point of intersection will be smaller than that of the second, as is sufficiently proved simply by the plot of Fig. 4. It is easily proved also that the condition for this result is always realized by the very nature of the law of demand. In consequence the root of equation (3) is always smaller than that of equation (4) ; or (as every one believes without any analysis) the result of competition is to reduce prices.

46. If there were 3, 4, ..., n producers in competition, all their conditions being the same, equation (3) would be successively replaced by the following :

$$D + 3p\frac{dD}{dp} = 0, \ D + 4p\frac{dD}{dp} = 0, \ \cdots \ D + np\frac{dD}{dp} = 0 \, ;$$

and the value of p which results would diminish indefinitely with the indefinite increase of the number n.

In all the preceding, the supposition has been that natural limitation of their productive powers has not prevented producers from choosing each the most advantageous rate of production. Let us now admit, besides the n producers, who are in this condition, that there are others who reach the limit of their productive capacity, and that the total production of this class is Δ ; we shall continue to have the n equations

$$(5) \begin{cases} f(D) + D_1 f'(D) = 0, \\ f(D) + D_2 f'(D) = 0, \\ \ \cdot \ \ \cdot \ \ \cdot \ \ \cdot \ \ \cdot \ \ \cdot \ \ \cdot \\ f(D) + D_n f'(D) = 0, \end{cases}$$

which will give $D_1 = D_2 = \cdots = D_n$, and by addition,

$$nf(D) + nD_1 f'(D) = 0.$$

But $D = nD_1 + \Delta$, whence

$$nf(D) + (D - \Delta)f'(D) = 0,$$

or

$$D - \Delta + np\frac{dD}{dp} = 0.$$

This last equation will now replace equation (3) and determine the value of p and consequently of D.

47. Each producer being subject to a cost of production expressed by the functions $\phi_1(D_1)$, $\phi_2(D_2)$, $\cdots$, $\phi_n(D_n)$, the equations of (5) will become

$$(6) \begin{cases} f(D) + D_1 f'(D) - \phi_1'(D_1) = 0, \\ f(D) + D_2 f'(D) - \phi_2'(D_2) = 0, \\ \cdot \quad \cdot \quad \cdot \quad \cdot \quad \cdot \quad \cdot \quad \cdot \quad \cdot \\ f(D) + D_n f'(D) - \phi_n'(D_n) = 0. \end{cases}$$

If any two of these equations are combined by subtraction, for instance if the second is subtracted from the first, we shall obtain

$$D_1 - D_2 = \frac{1}{f'(D)}[\phi_1'(D_1) - \phi_2'(D_2)]$$

$$= \frac{dD}{dp}[\phi_1'(D_1) - \phi_2'(D_2)].$$

As $\dfrac{dD}{dp}$ is essentially negative, we shall therefore have at the same time

$$D_1 \gtrless D_2 \text{ and } \phi_1'(D_1) \lessgtr \phi_2'(D_2).$$

Thus the production of plant *A* will be greater than that of plant *B*, whenever it will require greater expense to increase the production of *B* than to increase the production of *A* by the same amount.

For a concrete example, let us imagine the case of a number of coal mines supplying the same market in competition one with another, and that, in a state of stable equilibrium, mine *A* markets annually 20,000 hectoliters and mine *B*, 15,000. We can be sure that a greater addition to the cost would be necessary to produce and bring to market from mine *B* an additional 1000 hectoliters than to produce the same increase of 1000 hectoliters in the yield of mine *A*.

This does not make it impossible that the costs at mine *A* should exceed those at mine *B* at a lower limit of production. For instance, if the production of each were reduced to 10,000 hectoliters, the costs of production at *B* might be smaller than at *A*.

48. By addition of equations (6), we obtain

$$nf(D) + Df'(D) - \Sigma \phi_n'(D_n) = 0,$$

or   (7) $$D + \frac{dD}{dp}[np - \Sigma \phi_n'(D_n)] = 0.$$

If we compare this equation with the one which would determine the value of *p* in case all the plants were dependent on a monopolist, viz.

(8) $$D + \frac{dD}{dp}[p - \phi'(D)] = 0,$$

we shall recognize that on the one hand substitution of the

term np for the term p tends to diminish the value of p; but on the other hand substitution of the term $\Sigma\phi_n'(D_n)$ for the term $\phi'(D)$ tends to increase it, for the reason that we shall always have

$$\Sigma\,\phi_n'(D_n) > \phi'(D)\;;$$

and, in fact, not only is the sum of the terms $\phi_n'(D_n)$ greater than $\phi'(D)$, but even the average of these terms is greater than $\phi'(D)$, *i.e.* we shall have the inequality

$$\frac{\Sigma\,\phi_n'(D_n)}{n} > \phi'(D).$$

To satisfy one's self of this, it is only necessary to consider that any capitalist, holding a monopoly of productive property, would operate by preference the plants of which the operation is the least costly, leaving the others idle if necessary ; while the least favoured competitor will not make up his mind to close his works so long as he can obtain any profit from them, however modest. Consequently, for a given value of p, or for the same total production, the costs will always be greater for competing producers than they would be under a monopoly.

It now remains to be proved that the value of p derived from equation (8) is always greater than the value of p derived from equation (7).

For this we can see at once that if in the expression $\phi'(D)$ we substitute the value $D = F(p)$, we can change $\phi'(D)$ into a function $\psi(p)$; and each of the terms which enter into the summational expression $\Sigma\,\phi_n'(D_n)$, can also be regarded as an implicit function of p, in virtue of the relation $D = F(p)$ and of the system of equations (6). In consequence the root of equation (7) will be the abscissa of the point of intersection of the curve

(a) $$y = \frac{F(x)}{F'(x)},$$

with the curve

(b) $y = nx - [\psi_1(x) + \psi_2(x) + \cdots + \psi_n(x)]$;

while the root of equation (8) will be the abscissa of the point of intersection of the curve (a) with one which has for its equation

(b') $$y = x - \psi(x).$$

As has been already noted, equation (a) is represented by the curve MN (Fig. 5), of which the ordinates are always real and positive ; we can represent equation (b) by the curve PQ, and equation (b') by the curve $P'Q'$. In consequence of the relation just proved, viz.,

$$\Sigma \, \psi_n(x) > \psi(x),$$

we find for the value $x = 0$, $OP > OP'$. It remains to be proved that the curve $P'Q'$ cuts the curve PQ at a point I situated below MN, so that the abscissa of the point Q' will be greater than that of the point Q.

This amounts to proving that at the points Q and Q', the ordinate of the curve (b) is greater than the ordinate of the curve (b') corresponding to the same abscissa.

Suppose that it were not so, and that we should have

$$x - \psi(x) > nx - [\psi_1(x) + \psi_2(x) + \cdots + \psi_n(x)],$$

or $(n - 1)x < \psi_1(x) + \psi_2(x) + \cdots + \psi_n(x) - \psi(x).$

$\psi(x)$ is an intermediate quantity between the greatest and smallest of the terms $\psi_1(x)$, $\psi_2(x)$, $\cdots$, $\psi_{n-1}(x)$, $\psi_n(x)$; if we suppose that $\psi_n(x)$ denotes the smallest term of this series, the preceding inequality will involve the following inequality :

$$(n-1)\,x < \psi_1(x) + \psi_2(x) + \cdots + \psi_{n-1}(x).$$

Therefore x will be smaller than the average of the $n-1$ terms of which the sum forms the second member of the inequality ; and among these terms there will be some which are greater than x. But this is impossible, because producer (k), for instance, will stop producing as soon as p becomes less than $\phi_k'(D_k)$ or $\psi_k(p)$.

49. Therefore if it should happen that the value of p derived from equations (6), combined with the relations

(9) $\quad D_1 + D_2 + \cdots + D_n = D$, and $D = F(p)$,

should involve the inequality

$$p - \phi_k'(D_k) < 0,$$

it would be necessary to remove the equation

$$f(D) + D_k f'(D) - \phi_k'(D_k) = 0$$

from the list of equations (6), and to substitute for it

$$p - \phi_k'(D_k) = 0,$$

which would determine D_k as a function of p. The remaining equations of (6), combined with equations (9), will determine all the other unknown quantities of the problem.

CHAPTER VIII

OF UNLIMITED COMPETITION

50. The effects of competition have reached their limit, when each of the partial productions D_k is *inappreciable*, not only with reference to the total production $D = F(p)$, but also with reference to the derivative $F'(p)$, so that the partial production D_k could be subtracted from D without any appreciable variation resulting in the price of the commodity. This hypothesis is the one which is realized, in social economy, for a multitude of products, and, among them, for the most important products. It introduces a great simplification into the calculations, and this chapter is meant to develop the consequences of it.

According to this hypothesis, in the equation

$$D_k + [p - \phi_k'(D_k)] \cdot \frac{dD}{dp} = 0,$$

the term D_k can be neglected without sensible error, which reduces the equation to

$$p - \phi_k'(D_k) = 0.$$

In consequence, the system of equations (6) of the preceding chapter will be replaced by

(1) $p - \phi_1'(D_1) = 0, \ p - \phi_2'(D_2) = 0, \ \cdots p - \phi_n'(D_n) = 0.$

These n equations, together with

$$(2) \qquad D_1 + D_2 + \cdots + D_n = F(p),$$

will determine all the unknown quantities p and D_1, D_2, ..., D_n.

If we conceive of all the equations of (1) as solved with reference to D_1, D_2, ..., D_n, the first member of equation (2) will become a function of p, which we can represent by $\Omega(p)$, so that this equation can be written in the very simple form

$$(3) \qquad \Omega(p) - F(p) = 0.$$

In the hypothesis under consideration, all the functions $\phi_k'(D_k)$ must be considered to increase with D_k. Otherwise the gross value of the product

$$pD_k = D_k \cdot \phi_k'(D_k)$$

would be less than the costs of production, which are

$$\phi_k(D_k) = \int_0^{D_k} \phi_k'(D_k)\, dD_k.$$

It is, moreover, plain under the hypothesis of unlimited competition, and where, at the same time, the function $\phi_k'(D_k)$ should be a decreasing one, that nothing would limit the production of the article. Thus, wherever there is a return on property, or a rent payable for a plant of which the operation involves expenses of such a kind that the function $\phi_k'(D_k)$ is a decreasing one, it proves that the effect of monopoly is not wholly extinct, or that competition is not so great but that the variation of the amount produced by each individual producer affects the total production of the article, and its price, to a perceptible extent.

As all the functions $\phi_k'(D_k)$ are supposed to increase with D_k, the expression for D_k derived from the equation $p = \phi_k'(D_k)$ is itself a function of p, increasing with p; the function which we have denoted by $\Omega(p)$ therefore must also necessarily increase with p.

51. This being established, if we conceive of all of the functions $\phi_k'(D_k)$ as being increased by the quantity u, as would take place in consequence of the establishment of a specific tax on the article, equation (3) would be replaced by

$$(4) \qquad\qquad \Omega(p - u) = F(p).$$

Let MN (Fig. 6) be the curve of which the equation is $y = F(p)$, a curve of which the characteristic feature is that its tangent always makes an obtuse angle with the positive axis of abscissas, p, or, in other words, that the derivative $F'(p)$ is always negative. Let PQ be the curve of which the equation is $y = \Omega(p)$, a curve of which the characteristic feature is, on the contrary, as we have just seen, that its tangent always forms an acute angle with the positive axis of abscissas. Finally, let $P'Q'$ be the curve of which the equation is

$$y = \Omega(p - u),$$

which is related to the curve PQ by the condition that the portions intercepted between these two curves, of all lines parallel to the axis of the abscissas, such as VS', are equal to u. The abscissas OT and OT' will denote, respectively, the roots of equations (3) and (4), roots which we can express by p_0 and p'. But it is evident from the shape of

the curve *MN*, that $OT' > OT$, or that $p' > p_0$, and, therefore, an increase in the cost of production will always be
followed by an increase in the price of the article. It is
equally apparent from the shape of the curves *PQ* and
P'Q', that *TT'* will always be smaller than *VS'*, or
$p' - p_0 < u$, *i.e.* that *in all cases the rise in price will be
less than the increase in cost.*

In the figure the supposition was that the curves *PQ* and
P'Q' turned their convex sides towards the axis of *y*, but
the result of the construction would be the same if the
curves turned their concave side towards this axis.

An analytical form can be given to the demonstration of
the theorem in question, but then, for ease in demonstration, it is necessary to consider the increase *u* and the
difference $p' - p_0 = \delta$ both as very small quantities, of which
the squares and higher powers can be neglected. In this
way equation (4) will reduce to

$$(\delta - u)\Omega'(p_0) = \delta F'(p_0).$$

But $\Omega'(p_0)$ is greater than o, and $F'(p_0)$ is less than o ;
wherefore δ is of the opposite sign to $\delta - u$, which involves
the two conditions,

$$\delta > o \quad \text{and} \quad \delta < u.$$

Moreover, this demonstration can be extended to any values
of *u* and of δ, according to the remarks in Article 32.

The more the curve *MN* approaches a straight line parallel to the axis of abscissas, or the less consumption varies
with the price, the more, it is plain, the difference $p' - p_0$
will approach to equality with *u*.

It further follows from this that the charges which fall on the article, even after leaving the producers' hands, will always diminish the price received by the producers.

52. To calculate the influence of this variation on the interests of producers and consumers, it is necessary to note that we shall have

$$[\phi_k{}'(D_k)]_0 = p_0 \quad \text{and} \quad [\phi_k{}'(D_k)]' = p' - u$$

if we designate by $[\phi_k{}'(D_k)]_0$ and $[\phi_k{}'(D_k)]'$ the values of $\phi_k{}'(D_k)$ which correspond to the value of D_k before and after the increase in cost u. But we have

$$p' - u < p_0, \text{ whence } [\phi_k{}'(D_k)]' < [\phi_k{}'(D_k)]_0;$$

and, therefore, since $\phi_k{}'(D_k)$ is a function of D_k, which increases with the variable D_k, we have

$$[D_k]' < [D_k]_0;$$

and, therefore, *a fortiori*, the product $(p' - u)[D_k]'$ is smaller than $p_0[D_k]_0$.

As a result of the increase in cost u, the producer (k) will lose :

1. The difference between the price p_0 and the price $p' - u$, on the quantity produced $[D_k]'$, or

$$(p_0 - p' + u)[D_k]';$$

2. The net profit which he was receiving on the quantity $[D_k]_0 - [D_k]'$, by which the increase in cost diminished the production, or

$$p_0([D_k]_0 - [D_k]') - ([\phi_k(D_k)]_0 - [\phi_k(D_k)]').$$

The total loss which he will suffer is therefore

$$p_0[D_k]_0 - (p' - u)[D_k]' - ([\phi_k(D_k)]_0 - [\phi_k(D_k)]').$$

This loss will become smaller as the function $\phi_k'(D_k)$, of which $\phi_k(D_k)$ denotes the integral, increases more rapidly between the limits of definite integration.

The total loss borne by the mass of producers will therefore be

$$p_0 D_0 - (p' - u)D' - \Sigma([\phi_k(D_k)]_0 - [\phi_k(D_k)]'),$$

the characteristic Σ denoting a summation with respect to the index k.

The same expression can be put in the form

$$uD' + p_0 D_0 - p'D' - \Sigma([\phi_k(D_k)]_0 - [\phi_k(D_k)]') \;;$$

but it cannot be proved, as in the analogous case in Article 38, that this quantity is greater than uD', which expresses the receipts from the tax, when u is a specific tax assessed on the article. On the contrary, as we always have

$$[\phi_k(D_k)]_0 > [\phi_k(D_k)]',$$

since $(D_k)_0 > (D_k)'$; if we have furthermore $p'D' > p_0 D_0$, *i.e.* if the value of p_0 is less than that which renders pD a maximum (see Article 24), the total loss suffered by producers will necessarily be less than uD'.

The loss borne by consumers, who buy the article regardless of the increase in price, will be equal to

$$(p' - p_0)D'.$$

This loss alone will be less than the receipts from the tax uD', since we have always $p' - p_0 < u$.

53. If the article were charged with a tax np, not specific, but proportional to the selling price, or burdened with new items of cost which operate as such a tax (see Article 41), the equation

$$p - \phi_k'(D_k) = 0$$

would be replaced by

$$(5) \qquad p - \phi_k'(D_k) - \frac{d(np \cdot D_k)}{dD_k} = 0.$$

When the differentiation indicated is carried out, this equation becomes

$$p - \phi_k'(D_k) - np - nD_k \cdot \frac{dp}{dD_k} = 0,$$

or more simply

$$p(1 - n) - \phi_k'(D_k) = 0 ;$$

inasmuch as, according to the hypothesis of indefinite competition, D_k being an inappreciable fraction of the total production D, $\frac{dp}{dD_k}$ is a quantity likewise inappreciable and negligible. Instead of equation (3) we shall therefore have

$$(6) \qquad \Omega[(1 - n)p] - F(p) = 0 ;$$

i.e. the price is increased by such a tax just as it would be if all the necessary expenses for production and distribution of the article were themselves increased in the ratio of $1 : \frac{1}{1 - n}$; a result absolutely similar to that which we obtained for the case of a monopoly. Thus a tax of this nature will affect each of the producers the more, the greater the expenses of production which he must bear.

The same observation would hold good, whether the

article were charged with a tithe or with a tax in kind proportional to the production, such as was the tax assessed by
the Spanish government on the gold and silver mines of
America. For, if we call n the ratio of the quantity levied
by the government to the total production, and if we suppose, as it is natural to do, that the tax does not alter the
law of consumption of the article, equations (5) and (6)
will be applicable to this hypothesis also.

54. Let us consider in particular one of these producers,
whose production is expressed by D_k. The net revenue of
this producer, or the income from his investment (the profit
to the manager being included in the operating expenses),
will have the value

$$(7) \qquad pD_k - \int^{D_k} \phi_k'(D_k) dD_k,$$

or, if we substitute for p its value $\phi_k'(D_k)$,

$$(8) \qquad \phi_k'(D_k) \cdot D_k - \int_0^{D_k} \phi_k'(D_k) \cdot dD_k.$$

This is the expression for the net return or income *in
money;* but if it were desired to have an expression of the
return *in kind*, or the quantity of the article produced, the
value of which represents the net return of the owner or
producer (k), the preceding expression should be divided
by $p = \phi_k'(D_k)$, and then we should have

$$(9) \qquad D_k - \frac{1}{\phi_k'(D_k)} \cdot \int_0^{D_k} \phi_k'(D_k) \cdot dD_k.$$

It must not be forgotten that the essential characteristic
of the function $\phi_k'(D_k)$ is that it increases with D_k.

II

If it happens that the price p, and consequently D_k, increase, all other circumstances remaining the same, it is evident that the rent in money will increase, but this is not so manifest and it has even been denied by economists as to rent in kind. But if we differentiate expression (9) with reference to D_k and if we make the differential coefficient equal to zero, so as to determine the value of D_k which renders this expression a maximum or a minimum, we shall find after reduction

$$\frac{d\phi_k{}'(D_k)}{dD_k} \cdot \int_0^{\cdot D_k} \phi_k{}'(D_k) \cdot dD_k = 0,$$

or more simply

$$\frac{d\phi_k{}'(D_k)}{dD_k} = 0,$$

a condition which cannot be satisfied, since the function $\phi_k{}'$, from its nature, increases constantly with D_k. Therefore expression (9) is incapable of any [maximum or] minimum value ; and since it evidently begins by being an increasing function, it must also constantly increase with D_k.

The rent will increase if all items of cost happen to fall for the individual producer (k) without any perceptible influence of this circumstance on the total quantity produced and on the price of the article ; but in case the decrease in cost affects all producers, the resulting fall in the price of the article may be so great that the income or rent of each individual producer may be diminished.

CHAPTER IX

OF THE MUTUAL RELATIONS OF PRODUCERS

55. Very few commodities are consumed in just the form in which they left the hands of the first producer. Ordinarily the same raw material enters into the manufacture of several different products, which are more directly adapted to consumption ; and reciprocally several raw materials are generally brought together in the manufacture of each of these products. It is evident that each producer of raw materials must try to obtain the greatest possible profit from his business. Hence it is necessary to inquire according to what laws the profits, which are made by all the producers as a whole, are distributed among the individuals in consequence of the law of consumption for final products. This short summary will suffice to make known what we mean by the influence of the *mutual relations* of producers of different articles, an influence which must not be confounded with that of the *competition* of producers of the same article, which has been analyzed in the preceding chapters.

To proceed systematically, from the simple to the complex, we will imagine two commodities, (a) and (b), which have no other use beyond that of being jointly consumed in the production of the composite commodity (ab) ; to begin with, we will omit from consideration the expenses caused by the production of each of these raw materials taken separately, and of the costs of making them effective, or of the formation of the composite commodity.

Simply for convenience of expression we can take for examples copper, zinc, and brass under the fictitious hypothesis that copper and zinc have no other use than that of being jointly used to form brass by their alloy, and that the cost of production of copper and zinc can be neglected, as well as the cost of making the alloy.

Let p be the price of a kilogram of brass, p_1 that of a kilogram of copper, and p_2 that of a kilogram of zinc; and $m_1 : m_2$ the proportion of copper to zinc in the brass, so that we should have, according to the hypothesis,

$$(a) \qquad m_1 p_1 + m_2 p_2 = p.$$

In general, let p, p_1, and p_2 denote the price of the unit of the commodity for the composite article (ab) and for the component commodities (a) and (b); and m_1 and m_2 the numbers of units, or of fractions of the unit, of each component commodity which enter into the formation of the unit of the composite commodity.

Furthermore, let

$$D = F(p) = F(m_1 p_1 + m_2 p_2)$$

be the demand for the composite commodity, and

$$(b) \qquad \begin{cases} D_1 = m_1 F(m_1 p_1 + m_2 p_2), \\ D_2 = m_2 F(m_1 p_1 + m_2 p_2), \end{cases}$$

the demand for each of the component commodities; if we *suppose* each of these to be handled by a monopolist, and

if we apply to the theory of the mutual relations of producers the same method of reasoning which served for
analyzing the effects of competition, we shall recognize that
the values of p_1 and p_2 are determined by the two equations

$$\frac{d(p_1 D_1)}{dp_1} = 0, \text{ and } \frac{d(p_2 D_2)}{dp_2} = 0,$$

of which the development gives

$$
\begin{cases}
F(m_1 p_1 + m_2 p_2) + m_1 p_1 F'(m_1 p_1 + m_2 p_2) = 0, & (1) \\
F(m_1 p_1 + m_2 p_2) + m_2 p_2 F'(m_1 p_1 + m_2 p_2) = 0 ; & (2)
\end{cases}
$$

no other system of values but the one resulting from these
equations being compatible with a state of stable equilibrium.

56. To prove this proposition, it is sufficient to show that
the curves $m_1 n_1$ and $m_2 n_2$ (which would be the plots of equations (1) and (2), under the hypothesis that the variables p_1
and p_2 represent rectangular coördinates) assume one or the
other of the dispositions shown by Figs. 7 and 8; for, if
that is admitted, we can show, as in Chapter VII, and, by
the same construction, sufficiently indicated by the dotted
lines of either figure, that the coördinates of the point of
intersection i (or the roots of equations (1) and (2)) are the
only values of p_1 and p_2 compatible with stable equilibrium.

We observe that when p_2 is equal to zero, p_1 has a
finite value Om_1, *i.e.* the one which renders the product
$p_1 F(m_1 p_1)$ a maximum. Thereupon, as p_2 increases, the
value of p_1, which will procure the greatest profit for producer (1), may continue to increase (as is the case in
Fig. 7), or to decrease (as is the case in Fig. 8) ; but, even
under the latter hypothesis, it can never become absolutely

equal to zero. The one case or the other will occur according to the form of the function F, and according as we find

$$\frac{[F'(p)]^2 - F(p) \cdot F''(p)}{2[F'(p)]^2 - F(p) \cdot F''(p)} \lessgtr 0.$$

In this inequality p denotes a function of p_1 and p_2, determined by equation (a).

But since equations (1) and (2) and the preceding inequality are symmetrical with reference to $m_1 p_1$ and $m_2 p_2$,
it will result that, whenever the form of the function F is
such that the ordinates p_2 of the curve $m_1 n_1$ continue to
increase for increasing values of p_1, then the abscissas p_1 of
the curve $m_2 n_2$ will go on increasing for increasing values
of p_2, so that the two curves will assume the disposition represented by Fig. 7. On the contrary, whenever the ordinates p_2 of the curve $m_1 n_1$ decrease for increasing values of
p_1, the abscissas p_1 of the curve $m_2 n_2$ will likewise go on
decreasing for increasing values of p_2, and then the two
curves will assume the disposition represented by Fig. 8.

57. As equations (1) and (2) can be considered as
determined, in consequence of the previous discussion, we
will remark that they yield at once

$$m_1 p_1 = m_2 p_2 = \tfrac{1}{2} p;$$

that is to say, that by the purely abstract hypothesis under
consideration, the profits would be equally divided between
the two monopolists; and, in fact, there would be no reason
why the division should be unequal, and to the profit of one
rather than of the other.

By addition of equations (1) and (2), we can deduce

(c) $$F(p) + \tfrac{1}{2}pF'(p) = 0,$$

while, if the interests of the two producers had remained undistinguished, p would have been determined by the condition that $pF(p)$ should be a maximum, *i.e.* by the equation

(c') $$F(p) + pF'(p) = 0.$$

To prove the accuracy of this distinction, exactly the same method of reasoning should be used that we took in treating of the competition of producers.

But there is this essential and very remarkable difference, that the root of equation (c) is always greater than that of equation (c'), so that the composite commodity will always be made more expensive, by reason of separation of interests than by reason of the fusion of monopolies. An association of monopolists, working for their own interest, in this instance will also work for the interest of consumers, which is exactly the opposite of what happens with competing producers.

Furthermore, the higher value of the root of equation (c) than of that of equation (c') can be shown by the same graphical construction which served to establish the opposite result in the chapter in which we treated of competition.

If we had supposed n commodities thus related, instead of only two, equation (c) would evidently have been replaced by

$$F(p) + \frac{1}{n}pF'(p) = 0 ;$$

from which we should conclude, that the more there are of

articles thus related, the higher the price determined by the division of monopolies will be, than that which would result from the fusion or association of the monopolists.

58. Such a form might be given to the function F that the curves represented by equations (1) and (2) would not intersect; for instance, if it were

$$F(p) = \frac{a}{b + p^2},$$

equations (1) and (2) would become

$$b - m_1^2 p_1^2 + m_2^2 p_2^2 = 0, \text{ and } b + m_1^2 p_1^2 - m_2^2 p_2^2 = 0,$$

and would represent two conjugate hyperbolas (Fig. 9), of which the limbs $m_1 n_1$ and $m_2 n_2$ have a common asymptote and cannot meet.

A passing note is sufficient for these peculiarities of analysis, which cannot have any application to actual events.

Another peculiarity of the same kind would appear if we suppose that the roots of equations (1) and (2) establish a value of p, and, consequently, a value of D which exceeds the quantity which one or other of the producers can furnish. Let Δ be the limit which D cannot exceed, because of a necessary limitation in the production of one of the component articles, and π the corresponding limit of p according to the relation $D = F(p)$. We shall therefore have

$$m_1 p_1 + m_2 p_2 > \pi;$$

i.e. the variables p_1 and p_2 can be the coördinates only of a point situated above the line $h_1 h_2$ (Fig. 10), which would have for its equation

$$m_1 p_1 + m_2 p_2 = \pi;$$

and consequently, if the point i, where the two curves m_1n_1 and m_2n_2 intersect, falls below the line h_1h_2, its coördinates cannot be taken for the values of p_1 and p_2. From this the conclusion can be drawn, if necessary by aid of the graphical construction indicated above, that the values of p_1 and p_2 are indeterminate, being subject only to this condition, that the points which would have the values of these variables for coördinates fall on the part k_1k_2 of the line, which is intercepted between the curves m_1n_1 and m_2n_2.

This singular result springs from an abstract hypothesis of the nature of those which we can discuss in this essay. It is very plain that in the order of actual facts, and where all the conditions of an economic system are accounted for, there is no article of which the price is not completely determined.

59. We will now take into consideration the costs of production of the two component articles, which we will represent by the functions $\phi_1(D_1)$ and $\phi_2(D_2)$. The values of p_1 and p_2 will now result from the two equations

$$(d) \begin{cases} \dfrac{d[\,p_1D_1 - \phi_1(D_1)\,]}{dp_1} = 0, \\[2mm] \dfrac{d[\,p_2D_2 - \phi_2(D_2)\,]}{dp_2} = 0, \end{cases}$$

which will become, by reason of equations (a) and (b),

(e_1) $\quad F(m_1p_1 + m_2p_2) + m_1F'(m_1p_1 + m_2p_2) \cdot [\,p_1 - \phi_1'(D_1)\,] = 0,$

(e_2) $\quad F(m_1p_1 + m_2p_2) + m_2F'(m_1p_1 + m_2p_2) \cdot [\,p_2 - \phi_2'(D_2)\,] = 0.$

From these we derive

$$m_1[\,p_1 - \phi_1'(D_1)\,] = m_2[\,p_2 - \phi_2'(D_2)\,],$$

or, by reason of the condition

$$\frac{m_1}{m_2} = \frac{D_1}{D_2},$$

$$D_1[p_1 - \phi_1'(D_1)] = D_2[p_2 - \phi_2'(D_2)].$$

From this it follows that if the functions $\phi_1'(D_1)$ and $\phi_2'(D_2)$ reduce to constants, the net profits of the two coöperating producers will be equal. But this will no longer be so in the more general case where the functions $\phi_1'(D_1)$ and $\phi_2'(D_2)$ vary respectively with D_1 and D_2. The net profits of the two producers will then be expressed by

$$D_1\left[p_1 - \frac{\phi_1(D_1)}{D_1}\right] \text{ and } D_2\left[p_2 - \frac{\phi_2(D_2)}{D_2}\right];$$

so that if we have, for instance,

$$\phi_1'(D_1) > \frac{\phi_1(D_1)}{D_1} \text{ and } \phi_2'(D_2) < \frac{\phi_2(D_2)}{D_2},$$

the net profit of producer (1) will be greater than that of producer (2). From equation (a) and equations (e_1) and (e_2) there can further be deduced

$$(f) \quad 2 F(p) + F'(p)[p - m_1\phi_1'(D_1) - m_2\phi_2'(D_2)] = 0,$$

$$m_1 p_1 = \tfrac{1}{2}[p + m_1\phi_1'(D_1) - m_2\phi_2'(D_2)],$$

and $\quad m_2 p_2 = \tfrac{1}{2}[p - m_1\phi_1'(D_1) + m_2\phi_2'(D_2)].$

But if there had been a fusion of monopolies, equation (f) would have been replaced by

$$(f') \quad F(p) + F'(p)[p - m_1\phi_1'(D_1) - m_2\phi_2'(D_2)] = 0.$$

By recourse to the graphic representation which has served us for similar cases, it will easily be recognized that the root of equation (f) is greater than that of equation (f'), and, therefore, that an increase in price is the result of separation of the monopolies.

60. Up to this point we have neglected to account for the expenses involved in putting the raw materials to use in the formation of the resultant article, as well as the transportation of this resultant commodity to the market where it is consumed, the taxes which may be imposed on it, etc.

But if we suppose that these expenses are proportional to the quantity turned out, which is ordinarily the case, and that the sum of these expenses, for each unit of the resultant article, is expressed by the constant h, equation (a) will be replaced by

$$p = m_1 p_1 + m_2 p_2 + h,$$

and instead of equation (f) we shall have

$$2\,F(p) + F'(p)[p - h - m_1 \phi_1'(D_1) - m_2 \phi_2'(D_2)] = 0.$$

Thus the result will be the same as if the expenses had been borne directly by producers (1) and (2), and as if the burden of these expenses had been divided between them in the ratio of m_1 to m_2.

61. By a less restricted hypothesis than the one which we have considered till now, each of the component articles is susceptible of various uses besides that of coöperating in the formation of the composite article. Let $F(p)$ be, as before, the demand for the composite article, and $F_1(p_1)$ and $F_2(p_2)$ the demand for article (1) and that for article (2), for other uses than that of coöperating in the production of the com-

posite article. The values of p_1 and p_2 will still be given by
the equations (d), but we shall have

$$D_1 = F_1(p_1) + m_1 F(m_1 p_1 + m_2 p_2),$$

and $\qquad D_2 = F_2(p_2) + m_2 F(m_1 p_1 + m_2 p_2),$

by reason of which the equations (d) become

$$F_1(p_1) + m_1 F(m_1 p_1 + m_2 p_2)$$
$$+ [F_1'(p_1) + m_1^2 F'(m_1 p_1 + m_2 p_2)] [p_1 - \phi_1'(D_1)] = 0,$$
$$F_2(p_2) + m_2 F(m_1 p_1 + m_2 p_2)$$
$$+ [F_2'(p_2) + m_2^2 F'(m_1 p_1 + m_2 p_2)] [p_2 - \phi_2'(D_2)] = 0.$$

These expressions thus become too complicated to make
it easy to derive any general consequences from them.
Without further delay we will therefore pass on to a case
far more important, and which can easily be treated in as
general a manner as is desired. This is the case where
each of the two articles concurrently used is produced under
the influence of unlimited competition.

62. According to the theory developed in Chapter VIII,
we now obtain two series of equations :

$$(a_1) \begin{cases} p_1 - \bar{\phi}_1' D_1 = 0, \\ p_1 - \bar{\phi}_2' D_2 = 0, \\ \cdots \cdots \cdots \\ p_1 - \bar{\phi}_n' \bar{D}_n = 0 ; \end{cases} \qquad (a_2) \begin{cases} p_2 - \bar{\bar{\phi}}_1' \bar{\bar{D}}_1 = 0, \\ p_2 - \bar{\bar{\phi}}_2' \bar{\bar{D}}_2 = 0, \\ \cdots \cdots \cdots \\ p_2 - \bar{\bar{\phi}}_n' \bar{D}_n = 0. \end{cases}$$

Over the letters ϕ and D we set one or two horizontal
lines according as they relate to article (1) or article (2).
The subscripts to these letters serve to distinguish the producers in each of the two series.

Together with the equations of (a_1) and (a_2) the two following equations should be considered :

(b_1) $\overline{D}_1 + \overline{D}_2 + \cdots + \overline{D}_n = F_1(p_1) + m_1F(m_1p_1 + m_2p_2)$,

(b_2) $\overline{\overline{D}}_1 + \overline{\overline{D}}_2 + \cdots + \overline{\overline{D}}_n = F_2(p_2) + m_2F(m_1p_1 + m_2p_2)$.

If we deduce from the equations of (a_1) and (a_2) the values of $\overline{D}_1$, $\overline{D}_2$, ... and $\overline{\overline{D}}_1$, $\overline{\overline{D}}_2$, ... as functions of p, equations (b_1) and (b_2) will assume the forms

$$(3) \qquad \Omega_1(p_1) = F_1(p_1) + m_1F(m_1p_1 + m_2p_2),$$

$$(4) \qquad \Omega_2(p_2) = F_2(p_2) + m_2F(m_1p_1 + m_2p_2),$$

in which $\Omega_1(p_1)$ denotes a function of p_1 which increases with p_1, and $\Omega_2(p_2)$ another function of p_2 which increases with p_2.

Suppose that the production of article (1) is subjected to an increase of expense u, such as would result from a specific tax ; the values of p_1 and p_2, which before the increase in expense were determined by equations (3) and (4), will become $p_1 + \delta_1$ and $p_2 + \delta_2$, and we shall have, to determine δ_1 and δ_2, the equations

(5) $\Omega_1(p_1 + \delta_1 - u)$

    $= F_1(p_1+\delta_1) + m_1F(m_1p_1 + m_2p_2 + m_1\delta_1 + m_2\delta_2)$,

(6) $\Omega_2(p_2 + \delta_2)$

    $= F_2(p_2+\delta_2) + m_2F(m_1p_1 + m_2p_2 + m_1\delta_1 + m_2\delta_2)$.

If we admit that in comparison with p_1 and p_2, u, δ_1, and δ_2 are small fractions, of which the powers higher than the first can be omitted in our calculations, then equations (5) and (6) will become, in virtue of equations (3) and (4),

$$\delta_1\{\Omega'_1(p_1) - F_1'(p_1) - m_1^2 F'(m_1 p_1 + m_2 p_2)\}$$
$$- \delta_2 m_1 m_2 F'(m_1 p_1 + m_2 p_2) = u\Omega_1'(p_1),$$

and $- \delta_1 m_1 m_2 F'(m_1 p_1 + m_2 p_2)$
$$+ \delta_2\{\Omega_2'(p_2) - F_2'(p_2) - m_2^2 F'(m_1 p_1 + m_2 p_2)\} = 0.$$

To simplify the notation, we will write Ω_1' instead of $\Omega_1'(p_1)$, F' instead of $F'(m_1 p_1 + m_2 p_2)$, and so on throughout. Finally, let us put

$$Q = \Omega_1'\Omega_2' - \Omega_1'F_2' - \Omega_2'F_1' - m_2^2 F'\Omega_1' - m_1^2 F'\Omega_2'$$
$$+ F_1'F_2' + m_1^2 F'F_2' + m_2^2 F'F_1'.$$

From this and from the two preceding equations we can derive

$$(7) \qquad \delta_1 = \frac{u}{Q} \cdot (\Omega_1'\Omega_2' - \Omega_1'F_2' - m_2^2 F'\Omega_1'),$$

and (8) $\qquad \delta_2 = \dfrac{u}{Q} \cdot m_1 m_2 \Omega_1'F'.$

If we observe that the quantities Ω_1' and Ω_2' are essentially positive, whereas the quantities F', F_1', and F_2' are essentially negative, inspection of the values of δ_1 and δ_2 will now permit us to observe the following results :

1. δ_1 is of the same sign as u ; for $\dfrac{\delta_1}{u}$ is equal to a fraction, of which both numerator and denominator have all their terms positive.

2. δ_1 is smaller than u ; for the denominator of the afore-

said fraction contains all the terms of the numerator, and besides them a number of terms which are all positive.

3. δ_2 is of opposite sign to δ_1; for the denominator of the fraction $\dfrac{\delta_1}{u}$ is the same as that of the fraction $\dfrac{\delta_2}{u}$, and the numerator of this latter fraction is a negative quantity.

Although we only obtained these results by supposing u, δ_1 and δ_2 very small with reference to p_1 and p_2, it is easy to see that this restriction can be removed by supposing that any increase of expense, of whatever kind, takes place by a succession of very small increments. As the signs of the quantities Ω' and F' do not change in the passage from one state to the other, the relations which we have just found between the elementary variations u, δ_1, and δ_2 will also hold between the sums of these elements (Article 32).

In consequence, any increase in expense in the production of article (1) will increase the price of that article, but, nevertheless, so that the rise is less than the increase in expense; and at the same time the price of article (2) will fall.

It would be easy to show the necessity of all these results by methods of reasoning, independent of the preceding calculations. If article (1) did not rise in price when affected by an increase in cost, the producers of it would be obliged to restrict their output to avoid a loss, and it is impossible that the price should fail to increase when the quantity delivered diminishes. The article must rise therefore, and must rise less than the increase in cost, as otherwise the producers would have no reason for restricting their output. Finally, since there results a smaller consumption of article (1), as well for the manufacture of the composite article as for all other uses, there must also result a smaller consumption or production of article (2); and, as this article is not subjected to an increase in the cost of production, the restriction of production for this article can only be caused by a decrease in the price.

The variation in the price of the composite article, resulting from the opposite variations δ_1 and δ_2 in the prices of the component articles, is equal to $m_1\delta_1 + m_2\delta_2$, and from equations (7) and (8) we obtain

$$m_1\delta_1 + m_2\delta_2 = m_1 u \cdot \frac{\Omega_1'(\Omega_2' - F_2')}{Q}.$$

It results from this expression that the variation in the price of the composite article is of the same sign as u and δ_1, and that it is less than $m_1 u$, which is as it should be, on account of the fall in the price of article (2).

If we suppose any number of articles used concurrently, it could be demonstrated in the same manner, and by calculations which would offer no other difficulty than their length, (1) that an increase in cost occurring in the production of one of the articles, raises the price of this article and that of the composite article, and causes a fall in the prices of all the other component articles; (2) that the increase in the price of the article affected is less than the increase in cost or than the tax laid upon it.

63. Let us now consider the case where the increase in cost u falls directly on the composite article, whether it is a specific tax imposed on this article, on an increase occurring in the cost of distribution of the article to consumers. Equations (3) and (4) will be replaced by

$$\Omega_1(p_1+\delta_1)=F_1(p_1+\delta_1)+m_1F(m_1p_1+m_2p_2+m_1\delta_1+m_2\delta_2+u),$$

and

$$\Omega_2(p_2+\delta_2)=F_2(p_2+\delta_2)+m_2F(m_1p_1+m_2p_2+m_1\delta_1+m_2\delta_2+u);$$

and these, when treated as were equations (5) and (6), will give

$$\delta_1\Omega_1'=\delta_1F_1'+m_1^2\delta_1F'+m_1m_2\delta_2F'+m_1uF',$$

and $\quad \delta_2\Omega_2'=\delta_2F_2'+m_1m_2\delta_1F'+m_2^2\delta_2F'+m_2uF';$

from which we derive

$$\delta_1=\frac{um_1F'(\Omega_2'-F_2')}{Q},$$

and $\qquad \delta_2=\frac{um_2F'(\Omega_1'-F_1')}{Q},$

in which the polynomial represented by Q is composed of the same terms as in the preceding article.

From these expressions we easily conclude, in virtue of the signs of the quantities Ω' and F' :

1. That both δ_1 and δ_2 are of the opposite sign to u.

2. That the quantity $m_1\delta_1+m_2\delta_2$ is numerically less than u.

Moreover, the variations δ_1 and δ_2 in the prices of the component articles are mutually connected by this very simple relation :

$$\frac{\delta_1}{\delta_2}=\frac{m_1(\Omega_2'-F_2')}{m_2(\Omega_1'-F_1')},$$

which is independent of the function F. Consequently, any increase of expense, or any tax which affects the composite article, will lower the prices of the component commodities, and at the same time will raise the price of the

1

composite article, but by a quantity less than u, since this rise in price will be expressed by

$$u + m_1\delta_1 + m_2\delta_2,$$

and since $m_1\delta_1 + m_2\delta_2$ is, as we have just seen, numerically less than u, and of opposite sign.

These results can readily be generalized, whatever the number and kind of the component commodities, so long as they are produced under the influence of unlimited competition. They are worthy of serious consideration, as they have all the certainty of mathematical theorems, without being such as must, on that account, be excluded from the number of practical truths.

64. Let us go on to the case where article (2) has a limit to its production, so that the value of p_2 derived from equations (3) and (4) would correspond to a demand for this article which its producers could not satisfy. If we denote by Δ_2 this limit of production, the values of p_1 and p_2 will be determined by the system of equations

$$\Omega_1(p_1) = F_1(p_1) + m_1F(m_1p_1 + m_2p_2),$$

and $$\Delta_2 = F_2(p_2) + m_2F(m_1p_1 + m_2p_2).$$

Under these circumstances there will be no change in the equations which determine the values of p_1 and p_2, if we suppose that there falls on article (2) a tax, or an increase in the cost of production, denoted by u ; consequently these values will remain the same, and the entire increase in the cost will be borne by the producers of (2), without any loss resulting to the consumers of the component commodities, or of the composite article.

If the tax u falls on article (1), both of the old prices p_1 and p_2 will vary, and may be represented by $p_1 + \delta_1$ and $p_2 + \delta_2$. Equations (5) and (6) are applicable to this case by replacing the function $\Omega_2(p_2 + \delta_2)$ in the second of these equations by the constant Δ_2, which amounts to supposing the derivative Ω_2' equal to zero in the formulas derived from these equations.

Thus, under the hypothesis that the variations u, δ_1, and δ_2 can be treated as very small quantities, we shall have :

$$\delta_1 = \frac{-u\Omega_1'(F_2' + m_2^2 F')}{R},$$

and
$$\delta_2 = \frac{u m_1 m_2 \Omega_1' F'}{R},$$

$$\frac{\delta_1}{\delta_2} = -\frac{F_2' + m_2^2 F'}{m_1 m_2 F'},$$

$$m_1\delta_1 + m_2\delta_2 = \frac{-u m_1 \Omega_1' F_2'}{R};$$

in which the composition of the polynomial R is given by the auxiliary equation

$$R = -\Omega_1'(F_2' + m_2^2 F') + F_1' F_2' + m_1^2 F' F_2' + m_2^2 F' F_1'.$$

From these equations are derived the following consequences, which are applicable to all values of the variations u, δ_1, and δ_2 :

1. δ_1 is of the same sign as u, and numerically smaller ; the article affected by the tax increases in price, but by an amount less than the tax, so that there will be a diminution in the quantity produced and in the income of its producers ;

2. δ_2 is of opposite sign to u, so that the article which is not directly affected by the tax falls in price, to the disadvantage of the producers of this article, even though the quantity produced does not vary;

3. $m_1\delta_1 + m_2\delta_2$ is of the same sign as u; thus the composite article will rise in price, the rise of the taxed article more than compensating for the fall of the other article.

It would be found in the same way that the prices of both component articles would fall if the tax or the increase in cost bears directly on the resultant article.

65. Let us now suppose that for some reason the limit Δ_2 changes and becomes $\Delta_2 + v_2$ without the occurrence of any change in the cost of production. Treating, according to our method, the variation v_2 and the resulting variations δ_1 and δ_2 to begin with as very small, we shall have:

$$\delta_1 = v_2 \cdot \frac{-m_1 m_2 F'}{R},$$

$$\delta_2 = v_2 \cdot \frac{-(\Omega_1' - F_1' - m_1^2 F')}{R},$$

$$m_1\delta_1 + m_2\delta_2 = v_2 \cdot \frac{-m_2(\Omega_1' - F_1')}{R}.$$

From these expressions we conclude that whatever the extent of the variations, raising the limit Δ_2 depresses the price of article (2), and raises the price of article (1), but in a less degree, so that it brings about a fall in the price of the resultant article.

CHAPTER X

OF THE COMMUNICATION OF MARKETS

66. The perfecting of commerce and of means of transportation, and the abolition of prohibitory laws or restrictive
taxes, may put into communication markets which were previously isolated from each other, either wholly or only with
reference to certain commodities. The object of this chapter is to study the principal consequences which the establishment of such communication may involve.

It is evident that an article capable of transportation
must flow from the market where its value is less to the
market where its value is greater, until this difference in
value, from one market to the other, represents no more
than the cost of transportation.

By cost of transportation must be understood, not only
the price of necessaries and the wages of the agents by
whom the transportation is mechanically carried on, but also
insurance premiums, and the profits of the merchant, who
ought to obtain in his business the interest on the capital
employed and a proper return for his industry.

To compare the values of the commodity in the two
markets, it is necessary to consider not only the prices of
this article in money, but also the rate of exchange between
the two markets, or, in technical terms, between the two

places, which may be respectively regarded as the commercial centres of the markets in question. For instance, if we take for our unit of value the value of one gram of silver in market *A*, the value of the commodity in market *B*, expressed in grams of silver, must be multiplied by the coefficient of exchange from *A* to *B* (Chapter III) ; and if this reduced value, added to the cost of transportation, gives a smaller sum than the value of the commodity in grams of silver in market *A*, then only will the transportation of the commodity from *B* to *A* take place.

67. It would be a complicated problem, and at the same time one of very little interest for economic theory, to determine the influence of the communication of markets on the price of an article which is the subject of a monopoly, as well in the importing as in the exporting market. It is easy to see that under any such hypothesis the effects of competition would be combined with those which result properly from the communication of markets; and it is simpler, as well as more important, to consider directly the case where the effects of monopoly are extinguished, *i.e.* where the production of the article in both markets is ruled by the laws of unlimited competition.

It is manifest in this case, as the production must always increase in the exporting market, that the price of the commodity will be higher there than before the outflow; and reciprocally, as the price must fall in the importing market, the quantity produced there will be smaller.

Before communication, the prices p_a and p_b in the two markets *A* and *B* were determined by equations of the *form*

$$(1) \begin{cases} \Omega_a(p_a) = F_a(p_a), \\ \Omega_b(p_b) = F_b(p_b), \end{cases}$$

in which the characteristics F and Ω have the signification which was attributed to them in Chapter VIII, and letters placed as indices at the foot of these characteristics serve to distinguish the functions which refer to market A from those which are relative to market B.

After communication, these two equations are to be replaced by the following,

$$(2) \quad \Omega_a(p_a') + \Omega_b(p_a' + \epsilon) = F_a(p_a') + F_b(p_a' + \epsilon),$$

in which p_a' represents the price in the exporting market A, and ϵ the cost of transportation from A to B.

68. One of the interesting questions which can be proposed is to know whether the communication of markets always increases the total production, or, in other words analytically, whether we shall find in all cases

$$(3) \quad F_a(p_a') + F_b(p_a' + \epsilon) > F_a(p_a) + F_b(p_b).$$

To settle this question in the negative, we have only to consider a particular case, which renders comparison of equations (1) and (2) more easy ; namely, the case where the quantities p_a, p_b, and p_a' only vary by quantities so small that, for an approximate calculation, it is possible to neglect the squares and higher powers of these differences.

Let

$$p_a' = p_a + \delta \text{ and } p_b = p_a + \omega,$$

whence, therefore,

$$p_a' + \epsilon = p_b + \delta + \epsilon - \omega.$$

We must suppose $\omega > \epsilon$, as otherwise the establishment of communication would not determine a flow from A to B.

By applying to equation (2) the method of substitution, development, and reduction, of which we have already given many examples, this equation will become

(4) $\delta\{\Omega_a'(p_a) - F_a'(p_a)\} = (\delta + \epsilon - \omega)\{F_b'(p_b) - \Omega_b'(p_b)\}$;

and from the signs which are the essential characteristics of the functions F' and Ω' it is easy hence to deduce :

1. That δ is of the same sign as $\omega - \epsilon$, and consequently positive ;

2. That we have $\delta < \omega - \epsilon$; which otherwise very evidently results from the fact that communication must raise the price of the commodity in the exporting market and depress it in the importing market.

Substituting now their values for p_a' and $p_a' + \epsilon$ in inequality (3), this becomes, after making the reductions,

$$\delta \cdot F_a'(p_a) + (\delta + \epsilon - \omega) F_b'(p_b) > 0.$$

If from equation (4) we derive the value of $(\delta + \epsilon - \omega)$, and cancel the common factor δ, which is positive, the preceding inequality will become

$$F_a'(p_a) + \frac{F_b'(p_b) \cdot \{\Omega_a'(p_a) - F_a'(p_a)\}}{F_b'(p_b) - \Omega_b'(p_b)} > 0,$$

or more simply, by eliminating the denominator, and changing the sign of the inequality because the denominator is negative,

(5) $\qquad F_b'(p_b) \cdot \Omega_a'(p_a) - F_a'(p_a) \cdot \Omega_b'(p_b) < 0.$

It is evident that this inequality, and consequently inequality (3), may or may not be satisfied according to the numerical relations of the functions F' and Ω'.

There is therefore no contradiction involved in admitting that the communication of markets diminishes the total production.

And, reciprocally, the isolation of markets may be a cause which increases the quantity of an article delivered for consumption. We intend here only to determine this fact, without pretending, which would be absurd, to contradict the opinion which has been very generally formed, of the advantages for the community procured by improvements in the means of communication or by the extension of markets. This question will be the subject of a thorough discussion further on.

It is well to remark that to make applicable the approximate formulas which we have just been using, it is not necessary that the quantities ω and ϵ should be very small with reference to the original prices p_a and p_b: it is enough that the differences δ and $\omega - \epsilon$ should be very small with reference to p_a.

69. Not only the quantity produced, but also the total value of the quantity produced, may, according to circumstances, increase or diminish in consequence of communication of markets. In fact, if we admit, what implies no contradiction, that the value of p_a is greater than the value of p, which would render the function $pF_a(p)$ a maximum, and, on the other hand, that the value of p_b is less than that which would render the function $pF_b(p)$ a maximum, then, since we have

$$p_a' > p_a, \text{ and } p_a' + \epsilon < p_b,$$

we shall also have, according to the tendency of these functions,

$$p_a' F_a(p_a') < p_a F_a(p_a),$$

and $(p_a' + \epsilon) F_b(p_a' + \epsilon) < p_b F_b(p_b),$

and *a fortiori*

$$p_a' F_a(p_a') + (p_a' + \epsilon) F_b(p_a' + \epsilon) < p_a F_a(p_a) + p_b F_b(p_b).$$

In general, the preceding inequality will or will not be satisfied, according to the numerical relations of the quantities which enter into the inequality.

70. A tax on exportation or on importation will produce the same effects as an increase in the cost of transportation, equal to the amount of the tax. Let us denote simply by p the price of the commodity which was established in the exporting market before the tax, or the root of the equation

$$\Omega_a(p) + \Omega_b(p + \epsilon) = F_a(p) + F_b(p + \epsilon).$$

Let u be the tax, which we will at first suppose to be a very small number with reference to p and $p + \epsilon$; then $p' = p + \delta$ will be the value of p which results as a consequence of the tax, while the development of the equation

$$\Omega_a(p + \delta) + \Omega_b(p + \delta + \epsilon + u)$$
$$= F_a(p + \delta) + F_b(p + \delta + \epsilon + u),$$

in which we only retain the first powers of the variations δ and u, will give us

$$(6) \begin{cases} \delta = -(\epsilon + u)\dfrac{\Omega_b'(p) - F_b'(p)}{\Omega_a'(p) - F_a'(p) + \Omega_b'(p) - F_b'(p)}, \\ \delta + u = \dfrac{u[\Omega_a'(p) - F_a'(p)] - \epsilon[\Omega_b'(p) - F_b'(p)]}{\Omega_a'(p) - F_a'(p) + \Omega_b'(p) - F_b'(p)}. \end{cases}$$

error in this formula, described on page ,

From these expressions the following conclusions are·
derived :

1. δ will be a negative quantity, and numerically smaller
than $\epsilon + u$; *i.e.* the tax will always cause the commodity to
fall in the exporting market, by a quantity which may be
greater than the tax itself, but will always be smaller than
the sum of the cost of transportation and the tax. All conditions being otherwise the same, the more considerable the
cost of transportation, the more the tax will affect the price
in the exporting market.

2. $\delta + u$ will be a positive or a negative quantity according as

$$\frac{u}{\epsilon} \gtrless \frac{\Omega_b'(p) - F_b'(p)}{\Omega_a'(p) - F_a'(p)},$$

and consequently may increase or diminish the price, according to circumstances, in the importing market.

In the ignorance in which we ordinarily are as to the
numerical relations which exist between the quantities
Ω_a', Ω_b', F_a', and F_b', the chances will be in favour of an
increase if the tax exceeds the cost of transportation, and,
on the contrary, they will be in favour of a decrease if the
cost of transportation exceeds the tax.

To pass from the hypothesis of a tax to that of a bounty
granted, whether on exportation or on importation, we
have only to consider u as negative in the equations of
(6) ; and then it is necessary to distinguish two cases,
according as u is a quantity numerically smaller or greater
than ϵ, *i.e.* according as the rate of the bounty is below or
above the cost of transportation.

In the first case δ remains a negative quantity, numerically smaller than the difference between the cost of transportation and the bounty. The article falls as well in the exporting as in the importing market.

In the second case the bounty raises the commodity in the exporting market by an amount less than the difference between the bounty and the cost of transportation, and it always lowers the commodity in the importing market.

71. In short, a duty always lowers the price in the exporting market, and, according to circumstances, may lower or raise it in the importing market. On the contrary, a bounty always lowers the price in the importing market, and, according to circumstances, may lower or raise it in the exporting market.

Within the limits here expressed, this proposition holds good for any values of p, ϵ, and u whatsoever, without any necessity of a restriction to a very small quantity in considering the variation u. The same method of reasoning which we made use of in Article 32 suffices to prove this.

It is, moreover, indifferent as to the determination of prices, and for the interests of producers and consumers in both markets, whether collection of the tax, or payment of the bounty, takes place at the departure of the commodity from the territory of A or at its entrance into the territory of B, although this is of great importance to the financial interests of the countries to which these territories belong.

It is needless to mention that any increase in the cost of transportation would act in the same way as a tax, and any decrease as a bounty.

72. It sometimes happens, when an internal revenue tax

is imposed on a commodity in the country of its origin, that in order to favour its exportation, the government reimburses or restores the amount of the impost to the merchant who exports the commodity. To estimate the results of this combination, let us observe that if the price p of the article in the exporting market were determined before imposition of the tax by the equation

$$\Omega_a(p) + \Omega_b(p + \epsilon) = F_a(p) + F_b(p + \epsilon),$$

then imposition of the tax u, without restitution of the impost when the commodity is exported, would involve a new price p', given by the equation

$$\Omega_a(p' - u) + \Omega_b(p' + \epsilon) = F_a(p') + F_b(p' + \epsilon) ;$$

and finally, if p'' is the price which is fixed in the exporting market, after reimbursement of the impost, p'' will be the root of the equation

$$\Omega_a(p'' - u) + \Omega_b(p'' + \epsilon - u) = F_a(p'') + F_b(p'' + \epsilon - u).$$

Let $p'' = p + \delta$. If we neglect the squares of δ and u, this last equation will give

$$(7) \quad \delta = u \cdot \frac{\Omega_a'(p) + \Omega_b'(p + \epsilon) - F_b'(p + \epsilon)}{\Omega_a'(p) + \Omega_b'(p + \epsilon) - F_a'(p) - F_b'(p + \epsilon)}.$$

It follows from this that δ is of the same sign as u, and numerically smaller, so that the combination of an internal revenue tax with restitution of the impost raises the commodity in the exporting market and lowers it in the importing market. This double effect can only be attained by an increase in the amount exported, and, in fact, as it is easy to see, the quantity exported, which has for its expression

$$\Omega_a(p) - F_a(p),$$

will become, after the variation in price caused by the above-mentioned combination,

$$\Omega_a(p + \delta - u) - F_a(p + \delta).$$

It remains, therefore, to be proved that

$$\Omega_a(p + \delta - u) - F_a(p + \delta) > \Omega_a(p) - F_a(p),$$

or, by developing and neglecting the squares of δ and u,

$$(\delta - u) \cdot \Omega_a'(p) - \delta \cdot F_a'(p) > 0.$$

By substituting for δ its value in terms of u, as given by equation (7), and suppressing the common factors, and carefully changing the sign of the inequality, when the factors suppressed are negative, this inequality becomes

$$-\Omega_b'(p + \epsilon) + F_b'(p + \epsilon) < 0,$$

which is evidently satisfied, on account of the signs of Ω' and F'.

These results may be extended to all values of δ and u.

73. In all the formulas of this chapter it would only be necessary to make $\Omega_a' = 0$ or $\Omega_b' = 0$, if the quantity produced in market A or market B should remain constant owing to the conditions of production.

CHAPTER XI

OF THE SOCIAL INCOME

74. So far we have studied how, for each commodity by itself, the law of demand in connection with the conditions of production of that commodity, determines the price of it and regulates the incomes of its producers. We considered as given and invariable the prices of other commodities and the incomes of other producers; but in reality the economic system is a whole of which all the parts are connected and react on each other. An increase in the income of the producers of commodity A will affect the demand for commodities B, C, etc., and the incomes of their producers, and, by its reaction, will involve a change in the demand for commodity A. It seems, therefore, as if, for a complete and rigorous solution of the problems relative to some parts of the economic system, it were indispensable to take the entire system into consideration. But this would surpass the powers of mathematical analysis and of our practical methods of calculation, even if the values of all the constants could be assigned to them numerically. The object of this chapter and of the following one is to show how far it is possible to avoid this difficulty, while maintaining a certain kind of approximation, and to carry on, by the aid of

mathematical symbols, a useful analysis of the most general questions which this subject brings up.

We will denote by *social income* the sum, not only of incomes properly so called, which belong to members of society in their quality of real estate owners or capitalists, but also the wages and annual profits which come to them in their capacity of workers and industrial agents. We will also include in it the annual amount of the stipends by means of which individuals or the state sustain those classes of men which economic writers have characterized as unproductive, because the product of their labour is not anything material or salable. Usage would doubtless permit the use of these words in a different acceptation ; but we think that the definition which has just been given is better qualified than any other for directing the line of argument toward accurate deductions and consequences capable of application.

Whenever a commodity is supplied for consumption, in the price for which it is sold there should be found shares pertaining to the incomes of landlords and of capitalists who furnished the raw materials and the instruments for utilizing them, and the profits and wages of the various industrial agents who have coöperated in producing the commodity and in bringing it to market. All the elements into which this price can be decomposed are distributed into various branches of the social income. In consequence, if p denotes the price of the unit of the commodity, and D the number of units annually supplied for consumption, the product pD will express the sum to the extent of which this commodity coöperates in making up the social income.

This part of the income, therefore, will increase or diminish in consequence of variations occurring in the price and consumption of the commodity, according as the product pD increases or diminishes ; and it will be at its highest possible point when the product pD or $pF(p)$ attains its maximum value.

75. Let us denote by p_0 and p_1 two different values of p, and by D_0 and D_1 the corresponding values of D. Let us further suppose, to make these ideas more precise, that

$$p_1 > p_0, \text{ and } p_1 D_1 < p_0 D_0,$$

so that an increase in price of the commodity involves a decrease in the social income, or at least in the portion of it pD.

This diminution of income will be differently subdivided, according to circumstances, between the various producers who coöperate in the creation of the commodity, whether by the use of their property or by personal work.

For the very reason that they have less income, they will have less money available for their own consumptions, which may affect the demand for other commodities, diminish the incomes of many other classes of producers, and cause by its reaction a new diminution in the social income. It is important to obtain an accurate idea of this reaction, which, vaguely considered, would seem to have no limit.

In consequence of the rise of the commodity, of which the price has passed from the value p_0 to the value p_1, those consumers who have continued to buy the commodity notwithstanding the rise have been obliged to withdraw from

x

the consumption of other commodities, for application to the demand for the commodity which has risen, a sum equal to $(p_1 - p_0)D_1$

On the other hand, those consumers whom the rise has deterred from demanding the commodity which they previously consumed have had at their disposal for other demands a portion of their incomes equal to $p_0(D_0 - D_1)$

Subtracting the first of these values from the second, we find for the remainder $\overline{p_0 D_0 - p_1 D_1}$

i.e. a sum exactly equal, as should be the case, to that by which the income of the producers of the commodity was diminished by the rise in price.

Thus, when we consider the producers and consumers of the commodity in question throughout the world, we find that the same annual amount remains available for the sum total of other commodities. The possibility then becomes apparent, that this amount may be so distributed that the demand for each of these commodities will remain the same as before ; and consequently so that no change will occur in the system of prices (except in the price of the commodity which has risen), nor in the system of incomes (except in the incomes of the producers who coöperate by the use of their property or by the personal industry in the production of the commodity which has risen).

76. As a matter of fact, of course this exact distribution is not admissible, and in general, on the contrary, it must be the case, that a perturbation experienced by one element of the system makes itself felt from that to the next, and by reaction throughout the entire system. Nevertheless, since

the variation occurring in the price of commodity A, and in the income of its producers, leaves intact the sum total of the funds applicable to the demand for the other commodities B, C, D, E, etc., it is evident that the sum diverted, by hypothesis, from commodity B, by reason of the new direction of demands, will necessarily be applied to the demand for one or several of the commodities C, D, E, etc. Strictly speaking, this perturbation of the second degree, which occurs in the incomes of the producers of B, C, D, etc., would react on the system in turn until a new equilibrium is established ; but, although we are unable to calculate this series of reactions, the general principles of analysis will show us that they must go on with gradually decreasing amplitude, so that it may be admitted, as an approximation, that a variation occurring in the incomes of the producers of A, while modifying the distribution of the remainder of the social income among the producers of B, C, D, E, etc., does not alter the total value of it, or only alters it by a quantity which is negligible in comparison with the variation $p_0 D_0 - p_1 D_1$, which is experienced by the incomes of the producers of A. The variation of the social income is thus reduced to $p_0 D_0 - p_1 D_1$, *with an error not exceeding quantities of the second degree*, to use the language of mathematicians.

Not only do the preceding considerations justify this simplification, which is strictly admissible whenever very small variations in the system of values are to be discussed, and without which it would be impossible to carry deductions any further, but admitting even that compensation does not take place in a particular case, i.e. that the variation $p_0D_0 - p_1D_1$ caused in the incomes of the producers of A differs sensibly from the resulting variation in the social income. As no reason appears why one rather than the other should be the greater or the smaller, it would still be permissible to suppose that compensation takes place whenever these considerations are not applied to a particular case, and when, on the contrary, only the average results, the general laws of the distribution of wealth, are under discussion.

Some readers will possibly object to the preceding arguments, that we have distinguished the consumers who cease to buy the commodity which rises from those who continue to buy in spite of the increase in price, without considering the consumers who only reduce the demand which they made for the commodity. But it is evident that for each consumer in this third category it is possible, theoretically, to substitute two others, who will be one in the first category, and the other in the second. The simplification which we have adopted, therefore, makes no real difference in the discussion.

77. According to the explanations which have just been given, and to which all analogous cases can be referred, we will suppose that the variation in the price of commodity A has diminished the social income by a value expressed by $p_0D_0 - p_1D_1$. Room must be made here for an essential observation, without which it would be impossible to give a suitable interpretation of the abstract theory of wealth, and one which gives the clue to many misunderstandings between speculative writers.

The consumers who demand commodity A, after as well

as before the variation in price, who pay $p_1 D_1$ for the same
quantity of the commodity for which they only paid $p_0 D_1$
before, are really in just the same situation as to fortune as
if the commodity had not risen and their in-
comes had been diminished by $(p_1 - p_0) D_1$

If, then, to this expression we add the
quantity which expresses the decrease in the
income of the producers of the commodity, *i.e.* $p_0 D_0 - p_1 D_1$
the sum $p_0 (D_0 - D_1)$
will express the *real* diminution of the social
income, of which the quantity $p_0 D_0 - p_1 D_1$ only expresses
the *nominal* diminution.

Let us note that this result coincides with that which
can be obtained directly, and in the simplest manner, by
considering that the rise in price has reduced from D_0 to
D_1 the annual production of the commodity, and by this
alone has destroyed annually a value equal to $p_0 (D_0 - D_1)$,
so that, in fact, the quantity D_1 which continues to be produced has increased in value, which reduces the loss borne
by the producers ; but that the benefit, which for them is to
be subtracted from the loss $p_0 (D_0 - D_1)$, is exactly balanced
by the loss which this rise causes to the consumers who
bear it, so that finally the loss for society must always be
valued at $p_0 (D_0 - D_1)$.

It must also be observed that the consumers who cease
buying commodity *A* after the advance, and who transfer to
commodities *B*, *C*, *D*, etc., a value exactly equal to the one
which has just been found, *i.e.* $p_0 (D_0 - D_1)$, experience a
loss in consequence of the variation in the price of *A*, by
being led to make a different use of this portion of their

incomes than the one which they preferred under the old
system of prices. But this kind of damage cannot be esti-
mated numerically, as can that which the producers bear
through diminution of their incomes, or the consumers by
the increase of the sum which they expend to buy the same
quantity of the commodity. Here comes in one of those
relations of order and not of size, which numbers can indicate indeed, but cannot measure. As our discussions only
consider measurable things, the product $p_0(D_0 - D_1)$ will
be, for the case in point, the measure of what we will call
the actual diminution of the social income, in contrast with
what we have called the nominal diminution.

78. If $p_0 D_0 < p_1 D_1$, p_0 remaining always smaller than p_1,
and consequently D_0 greater than D_1, the same considerations as those discussed above will prove that the social
income has nominally increased in consequence of the rise
of the commodity, and that it has increased by a quantity
sensibly equal to $p_1 D_1 - p_0 D_0$, or to the increase which
occurs in the incomes of the producers of the commodity
which has risen. But if, then, from the loss borne by the consumers, a loss equivalent to a diminution of in-
come, and of which, as before, the expression is $(p_1 - p_0) D_1$
we subtract the nominal increase of the social

income $p_1 D_1 - p_0 D_0$

the difference $p_0(D_0 - D_1)$

will give, as before, the measure of the **real**
diminution of the social income, although this income has
received a nominal increase.

It is plain that this nominal increase is very real for the
producers, among whom the value $p_1 D_1$ is divided ; but they

only obtain this advantage at the expense of consumers, whose losses more than compensate for the benefit received by the producers ; so that, for society considered throughout the world, there is an increase in the nominal income and a decrease in the actual income.

If, therefore, the question is of a commodity for which the cost of production is either nothing or insensible, the most favourable condition for a nominal increase in the social income would be for this commodity to fall into the hands of a monopolist, since the product pD would then reach its maximum value ; but whatever there is of paradox in such a proposition, vanishes when attention is paid to the distinction which has just been made between the nominal and the real variations of income.   Evidently, as the monopoly of such a commodity is divided between two, three, or more producers, the commodity will gradually fall in price, according to the formulas given in Chapter VII ; the consumption will go on increasing, and the social income, although nominally decreasing, will experience an actual increase ; as, in fact, common sense teaches that society can only gain by the weakening or extinction of such a monopoly.

79. Whenever a commodity, besides being subject to a cost of production, is under a monopoly, we can be sure that any tax or any increase of cost, by raising the price and reducing the consumption of the commodity, will cause to the social income, not only an actual, but also a nominal diminution.   In fact, if $\phi(D)$ is the function which measured the cost borne by the monopolist, and to which new expenses are now added, p_0 being the value which renders the function $pD - \phi(D)$ a maximum, we shall have

$$p_0 D_0 - \phi(D_0) > p_1 D_1 - \phi(D_1),$$

and since $\phi(D_0)$ is greater than $\phi(D_1)$, because D_0 is greater than D_1, therefore *a fortiori* $p_0 D_0 > p_1 D_1$.

But when a commodity, subject to a cost of production, is at the same time free from monopoly, a rise in price, due to an increase in the cost of production, while always diminishing the real value of the social income, may increase or diminish its nominal value, according as the initial value p_0 falls below or above the value π, which renders the product pD a maximum, and which would be, in fact, the price of the commodity if there were no cost of production, and if the commodity were under a monopoly. Liberation from monopoly tends to make p_0 smaller than π; but, on the other hand, the cost of production tends to raise p_0 above π. It is evident that, according to circumstances, one or the other of these causes which act in opposite directions will prevail; so both hypotheses $p_0 > \pi$ and $p_0 < \pi$ are equally admissible *a priori* (Article 24).

80. It is evident from the preceding, how it is possible that a tax on consumption nominally increases the social income, while it diminishes its actual value. When imposition of a tax i renders positive the quantity $p_1 D_1 - p_0 D_0$, which then expresses the nominal increase in income, the treasury collects a portion $i D_1$ of the value produced, $p_1 D_1$; but this part, which in our day no longer accumulates in the coffers of the treasury, whether it serves to pay the interest on the public debt, or whether it is spent in salaries or largesses, or whether it is used to buy finished products for *the public service*, still goes to create the incomes of several

classes of consumers. As regards taxes levied directly on income, the treasury, supposing that it has no foreign tributes to pay, only acts as an intermediate machine designed to change (to be sure, often in an oppressive and unjust manner) the distribution of the social income, without immediately changing the total value of it. With reference to taxes on consumption, the treasury plays this part of an intermediate machine for the portion iD_1 of the total value produced, which is destined to pay the tax, and besides this the tax causes a diminution expressed by $p_0(D_0 - D_1)$ in the real value of the social income.

81. For the same reason that an increase in the cost of production diminishes the real value of the social income, while diminishing or increasing the nominal income according to circumstances, a decrease in cost will always increase the real value of this income, while increasing or diminishing the nominal income, according to circumstances. Let us suppose that, in consequence of a reduction in the cost of production of commodity A, and of the fall in price which followed, the social income has nominally decreased by $\qquad p_0 D_0 - p_1 D_1$

The consumers, who made the demand for this commodity before the fall, will be in the same position as if the commodity had not changed in price, and the sum of their incomes had been increased by $\qquad (p_0 - p_1) D_0$

Subtracting the first expression from the second, we shall find for remainder the positive quantity $\qquad p_1 \overline{(D_1 - D_0)}$
which will express the real increase in social

income. The result would evidently have been the same if the fall in price had raised the nominal value of the social income, or if we had had $p_1D_1 > p_0D_0$; for then it would have been necessary to add to $(p_0 - p_1)D_0$ the positive quantity $p_1D_1 - p_0D_0$, which amounts to subtracting $p_0D_0 - p_1D_1$ as before.

Moreover, this result can be reached directly by an argument similar to that of Article 77. The fall in the price has raised the annual production of the commodity from D_0 to D_1, and by this alone has annually created a value equal to $p_1(D_1 - D_0)$. To be sure, the quantity D_0, which had already been produced previously, has fallen in price, to the disadvantage of producers; but this loss, which for them is to be subtracted from the profit $p_1(D_1 - D_0)$, is exactly balanced by the profit which the fall grants to those consumers who were buying and continue to buy the quantity D_0, so that, in the end, the real gain for society must always be valued at $p_1(D_1 - D_0)$.

In estimating the real increase in the social income caused by a fall in price, no account is made of the advantage for the new consumers of the commodity, which consists in employing a part of their incomes in a manner more to their taste; for this advantage is not capable of numerical appreciation, and is not a new source of wealth in itself, although it may finally lead to an increase in wealth, if the commodity A is the raw material of other products, or an instrument which serves for other products.

82. Hitherto we have supposed that a rise or fall in the cost of production, or imposition or remission of a tax, *caused an increase* or diminution of the price and conse-

quently a reduction or expansion of production, whereas the law of demand, *i.e.* the relation which exists between the quantities D and p, remained the same. But the direct argument, employed in Articles 77 and 81, would be equally applicable if the variations in the price and in the quantity produced resulted in a variation in the form of the function $F(p)$, which expresses the law of demand,—a change which might also result from an alteration in the tastes and needs of consumers, as well as from an alteration in the method of distribution of the social wealth. Let us admit, therefore, that in consequence of such an alteration, a portion h of the social income has been diverted from the demand for commodity A, and applied in a single lump to commodity B, so that the incomes of the producers of the other commodities C, D, E, etc., will not experience any alteration, or will only suffer negligible variations. Calling p_0 and D_0 the price and the demand for commodity A before the variation occurred, and p_1 and D_1 what these quantities become after the variation, we shall have

$$p_0 D_0 - p_1 D_1 = h.$$

In the same way, if we distinguish by primes the quantities relating to commodity B analogous to those relating to commodity A, we shall have

$$p_1' D_1' - p_0' D_0' = h,$$

and consequently

(1) $$p_0 D_0 - p_1 D_1 = p_1' D_1' - p_0' D_0'.$$

The social income will have experienced neither an increase nor a diminution in its nominal value; but on one side there will be a loss in its actual value expressed by

$$p_0(D_0 - D_1) ;$$

and, on the other hand, an actual gain expressed by

$$p_1'(D_1' - D_0') ;$$

so that the actual balance will be favourable or unfavourable according as we have

(2) $p_1'(D_1' - D_0') \gtrless p_0(D_0 - D_1),$

and proportionally more favourable or unfavourable according as the first member of the inequality varies further from the second member, while equation (1) continues to remain satisfied.

In virtue of equation (1), we can replace inequality (2) by the following :

$$(p_0' - p_1')D_0' \gtrless (p_1 - p_0)D_1.$$

It is easy to conceive that articles of luxury, of which the consumption is reserved to the wealthy classes of society, are generally characterized in the economic system by this property, that slight variations in the demand, or in the competition of purchasers, may cause very considerable variations in prices, because the wealthy man can readily triple or double the price which he sets on an article which strikes his fancy. On the other hand, it is observed that for articles of general consumption, but which nevertheless are not considered of prime necessity, slight variations in price correspond to considerable variations in the demands *or in the quantities* produced.

In consequence, the causes which tend to reduce the great inequalities in the distribution of wealth will tend to cause variations in the economic system, of which the average and general effect will be to increase the actual value of the social income.

This increase in actual value may be accompanied by an increase in nominal value, if commodity B, in favour of which the change in the direction of the demand takes place, is the raw material or an instrument in the production of new commodities. From this point of view, modifications in the economic system which favour increase of the labouring classes, by inducing more abundant production of the commodities necessary for them, tend also to an increase in the actual value of the social income, as we defined it — an income of which the wages of workingmen form an integral and most important part.

The commodities of prime necessity, which are the staples of food, seem to have this in common with objects of luxury, that enormous variations in price correspond to slight variations in the quantities produced, because the poorer classes find themselves forced to sacrifice all other demands to those for these commodities. But such sacrifices cannot be prolonged without causing violent disturbances in the constitution of the economic system and of the population; and, therefore, when only average values are considered, independently of temporary disturbances, it is found, even for the commodities of prime necessity, that great differences in the quantities produced correspond to slight variations in prices.

Just because a considerable temporary increase in the

prices of these commodities corresponds to slight differences in consumption, it results from our theory, as from
the plain admonitions of common sense, that such an increase causes a real reduction of the social income, even
when it nominally increases the value of it. But our theory,
which is always in agreement with common sense, shows
that a very different verdict must be given concerning any
progressive and secular advance which might affect the
commodities in question.

83. The same principles bring us to an analysis of what
happens when a new commodity, a new exchangeable value
rises, so to speak, to the surface of the economic system. A commodity N, which hitherto did not appear in
the circulation of wealth, is now created in all its parts, and
the quantity annually made or sold is valued at h. Buyers
of this commodity therefore direct from the demand for
the other commodities A, B, C, etc., a sum h drawn from
their incomes; but this sum is returned by the producers
of commodity N to the total of the demands for commodities A, B, C, etc. There is therefore no reason why
the former economic system, taken as a whole, should feel
any perturbations; it is a simple juxtaposition, so to speak,
which occurs; the social income, nominally and actually,
is increased by the sum h, which constitutes the income of
the producers of the new commodity.

It should be carefully noted under what conditions such
a result occurs, for it would be easy to imagine an hypothesis
which would lead to very different results. Supposing, for
instance, that an exchange occurs between producers of N
and M, so that the former, who enjoy an income h arising

from purchases by the latter of the new commodity, employ exactly this income in purchasing commodity M, and thus give rise to an increase corresponding with the value h in the production of this commodity; all the other elements of the economic system may have remained unchanged; but the social income will have increased, as well in nominal as in actual value, by twice the amount h; namely, by the entirely new income of the producers of N and by the increase in the income of the producers of M.

By thus giving attention to peculiar and, moreover, improbable hypotheses, which can be infinitely varied, the problem under consideration in this article would become entirely indeterminate. To make it admit of a determinate solution, it is necessary to start from the only probable hypothesis of the condition of commercial relations; it must be supposed that producers of the new commodity sell to any consumers, and spend the incomes which this market gives them, in purchases from any other producers, without intervention of any such conventions as those by which the craftsmen of a small town give their custom to each other, and without natural occurrence of results similar to those which would arise from such a convention.

But results of this kind may occur whenever producers are divided into great categories; as, for instance, when the class of landlords or managers of real estate is opposed to that of labourers dependent on their wages; and especially whenever the manner of distribution of wealth establishes a sharply defined distinction between these two classes. If the labouring population increases, or becomes more industrious, the products of its industry will be almost entirely consumed by the landowning class, and the reward of this industry will be almost wholly employed in making an outlet for the products of the earth and in encouraging and extending agricultural industry. The rich will see their wealth increase at the same time as, and even by reason of the fact that, they find means to satisfy new tastes. The social income, in which we include the wages of all workers as well as the incomes of all capitalists, will therefore increase in a more rapid progression on account of this particular, but this does not mean that the manner of distribution of wealth, by reason of which this particular is true, is preferable to others for the ultimate interest of the body politic.

If we omit these peculiar cases the discussion of which eludes our theory, and which, so to speak, disturb the foundations of the economic system, and if we consider what occurs in a state which approaches equilibrium, we find that putting in circulation a new commodity should have for a mean result to increase the social income by an amount just equal to the value of the quantity of this commodity annually produced.

84. Whether man seeks to create new products which shall render life pleasanter and lighten its burdens, or whether the refinements of social life by exciting new desires give value to articles not previously in request, the result will be the same from the standpoint of economic science, although the moralist and the statesman may give very different opinions as to the fate of a people, according as they observe luxury or industrious activity to prevail *among them.* It has been truly said that luxury enriches a

nation, in this sense that the social income is increased by putting in circulation new products which would not have come into use without luxury and the refinements of social life. It has also been said, with not less of truth, that luxury induces the ruin of a nation, not only in the moral and political sense, but also in the commercial acceptation of the word, when the production of articles of luxury can only take place at the expense of the production of other commodities which are the intermediate or direct instruments for further products.

Here should be introduced the distinction between unproductive and reproductive consumptions, if this distinction had not been made with all the clearness and all the developments desirable by Smith, and especially by J. B. Say. The man who economizes or capitalizes a portion h of his income diverts the sum h from the demand for commodities A, B, C, etc., which only offer him the enjoyment of an unproductive consumption, to apply it to the demand for commodities L, M, N, etc., which will be converted into instruments of production. The result of this new direction given to the demand will be to encourage certain callings and to discourage others, to increase the income of certain classes of producers at the expense of other producers ; but, in virtue of the principles already explained, when account is taken only of the average and general effects, the social income will remain the same. Later, and when the new productive property, which was created by the saving, begins to bear fruit, the former income will be increased by the income of the capital h. Of course, saving or capitalization cannot exceed certain limits, and

L

finally, the consumption known as unproductive is the regulator and object of the so-called productive consumption. What are the insuperable limits? What are the relations of unproductive to productive consumption? Theory cannot determine this *a priori;* but in practice, just because capital finds profitable investment, we know that a nation still remains where saving contributes to the progress of the public wealth at the same time that it satisfies individual inclinations to prudence or cupidity.

85. The social income may be nominally increased, both by the creation of new productive property, or the manufacture of a new circulating value ; and by a change in conditions which gives a small value to some article useful, but previously enjoyed gratuitously, and which therefore could have no value in exchange. Thus, there is no contradiction in supposing that the nominal value of the social income would increase, if substances with which nature has abundantly endowed us in quantities beyond our requirements, such as water, should become rare or should require expense for production ; or if the natural forces which every one freely uses, such as the motive power of the wind, should become susceptible of appropriation and a rent should have to be paid for them to the landlord. But whatever paradox exists in this statement disappears when the distinction is considered which we have made in this chapter between real and nominal value. It is unnecessary for us to enter into further developments for the sake of an objection which is purely speculative and to some extent scholastic.

86. We have to answer a much more specious objection *which applies to* what precedes. It will be said that when

the production of commodity A decreases, and falls for instance from D_0 to D_1, the value of the quantity $D_0 - D_1$ is not on that account wholly withdrawn from circulation; that the raw materials which went to its manufacture find another use at the expense of a reduction in price to find this use; that the workmen whose labour was employed in this occupation will lend their hands to other producers at the expense of a more or less important reduction in the rate of their wages; and finally that the capital employed in this operation will find another field, at the expense to the capitalists of reducing if necessary the rate of interest which they demand. At the first sight it may seem that we have not considered this essential condition, and that we have reasoned as if the reduction in the production of commodity A withdrew from circulation a value exactly equal to that of the quantity by which the production is reduced.

To show that we have not fallen into this error, let us suppose that one commodity M plays the part of raw material with reference to several commodities A, B, C, etc., which go directly into consumption. In the number of the producers of A should be included those of the producers of M who furnish one of the raw materials used in the manufacture of A (Article 74), to an extent corresponding with the amount which they furnish for this use. The same can be said concerning commodities B, C, etc. In consequence, the income of any producer of M may be decomposed into several parts, for the first of which he is ranked among the producers of A, for the next among the producers of B, and so on. If the reduction in the consumption of commodity A induces a greater production of commodity

B, the producer of M may find in the increased outlet for the manufacture of the composite commodity B, compensation for the loss which he suffers by the decrease in the outlet for the manufacture of the composite commodity A ; but there is nothing to prevent an imaginary substitution, for convenience in argument, for this producer of M of two producers M_1 and M_2, of whom the one furnishes only the raw material for the manufacture of commodity A, and the other for commodity B, so that M_1 is counted only among the producers of A, and M_2 among the producers of B. But in estimating the average results, we considered the transfer of the funds withdrawn from the demand for commodity A, to the demand for commodities B, C, etc. ; so that we have implicitly considered the essential condition, neglect of which would have given rise to the objection which we are endeavouring to refute in this article.

The remark just made concerning commodities, properly so called, which act as raw materials, is equally applicable to labourers' wages, and to the return on the capital which co-operates in the preparation of the composite commodities which are the final object of productive industry. When a labourer works first at the production of commodity A, and then at that of commodity B, after the reduction which occurs in the production of A, he should be ranked in the first place among the producers of A, and in the second among the producers of B ; the income of group A, which includes labourers' wages, is diminished, and that of group B increases ; with reference to the calculations under consideration, it is exactly as if the demand for labour increased *for the labourers on B* and diminished for the labourers on

A, without its being possible for the same workman to pass from the one employment to the other.

Finally, although we make continuous and almost exclusive use of the word *commodity*, it must not be lost sight of (Article 8) that in this work we assimilate to commodities the rendering of services which have for their object the satisfaction of wants or the procuring of enjoyment. Thus when we say that funds are diverted from the demand for commodity *A* to be applied to the demand for commodity *B*, it may be meant by this expression, that the funds diverted from the demand for a commodity properly so called, are employed to pay for services or *vice versa*. When the population of a great city loses its taste for taverns and takes up that for theatrical representations, the funds which were used in the demand for alcoholic beverages go to pay actors, authors, and musicians, whose annual income, according to our definition, appears on the balance sheet of the social income, as well as the rent of the vineyard owner, the vine-dresser's wages, and the tavern-keeper's profits.

CHAPTER XII

OF VARIATIONS IN THE SOCIAL INCOME, RESULTING FROM THE COMMUNICATION OF MARKETS

87. In Chapter X we investigated the effects of the communication of markets on the determination of prices and the incomes of producers; we now mean to take up, according to the same principles which underlay the theory developed in the preceding chapter, how communication, how commerce between two markets, or, if it is preferred, the exportation of commodities from one market to another, causes the value of the social income to vary, as well in the importing as in the exporting market.

This question derives an especially strong interest when commercial relations between different peoples are considered, as being essentially subject to the regulating action of governments. For the term *social income* there may then be substituted *national income*, which, however, will not denote the income which the government of a nation derives from taxation, and which serves to pay public expenses, but the sum total of individual incomes, of rents, of profits, and of wages of every kind, in the whole extent of the national territory.

Here we are evidently approaching the question, with a *view to which* all systems of political economy have, so to

speak, been constructed ; the question which for two cen-
turies has been discussed by theorists and by statesmen.
We have not the temerity to approach it from the statesman's standpoint ; but, on the other hand, we believe that
this question, when considered in its theoretical aspect, can
be reduced to very simple terms, of which the mere statement, by overthrowing false systems, opens the way to the
practical knowledge which essentially concerns the destiny
of nations.   It is on this account that the considerations
which we are here examining appear to us something more
than mere intellectual exercises or chimerical abstractions.

It will always be advantageous, by means of precise symbols and a more rigorous method of demonstration, to explain, in a few words, the difficulties raised by volumes of
controversy.

88.   Let us call A and B the exporting and importing
markets ; M the commodity which is exported from A to B ;
p_a and D_a the price and the demand for the commodity in
market A, at the time when for some cause, for instance on
account of a prohibition, exportation of the commodity
could not take place ; p_b and D_b the price and the demand
in market B at the same time ; p_a' and D_a' the price and
the quantity produced at A after establishment of communication ; p_b' and D_b' the price and the quantity produced at
B ; Δ the quantity consumed at A after communication, or
the demand of consumers at A corresponding to the price
p_a' ; and E the quantity exported, so that $D_a' = \Delta + E$.

The producers at A obtain an increase in income equal
to $p_a'D_a' - p_aD_a$.   We must suppose $p_a' > p_a$, $D_a' > D_a$, and
a fortiori, $p_a'D_a' > p_aD_a$.   In fact, the case where, in conse-

quence of a monopoly, communication of markets causes the price to fall, even in the exporting market, is too peculiar for us to delay over, and, moreover, nothing is easier than to modify the arguments which follow, so as to meet this special hypothesis.

The consumers of market A, who continue to buy commodity M, will withdraw from the portion of their incomes formerly devoted to the other commodities N, P, Q, etc., a value equal to $\qquad (p_a' - p_a)\lambda \quad (1)$

On the other hand, those whom the increase in price prevents from buying can add to the funds which they previously devoted to the demand for the commodities N, P, Q, etc., a value equal to $\quad p_a(D_a - \Delta) \quad (2)$

Finally, since market A disposes by export of a value equal to $p_a'E$, it will receive in return an equal value in some commodity, whatever it may be. By the fact of exportation, therefore, a value $\qquad p_a'E \qquad (3)$ is withdrawn from the demand for commodities N, P, Q, etc., on the home market, to be applied to the demand for commodities of foreign origin, and goes to make up the income of foreign producers. But, by adding quantities (1) and (3), and subtracting from the sum quantity (2), we obtain for result $p_a'D_a' - p_aD_a$ (on account of the relation $D_a' = \Delta + E$), *i.e.* a value exactly equal to that by which the income of the producers of commodity M has increased. Therefore the sum total of the funds available for the demand for commodities N, P, Q, etc., remains unchanged. We can therefore admit, thanks

to the hypothesis for simplification which has been sufficiently explained, that the national income at A, or the
sum total of the incomes of the producers at A, has
increased, in consequence of the exportation of commodity M, by a value exactly
equal to $\quad\quad\quad\quad\quad\quad\quad\quad p_a'D_a' - p_aD_a$

But this is only a nominal increase in income. The consumers who have paid at the
rate p_a' for the quantity of the
commodity denoted by Δ, instead of paying at the rate p_a,
are precisely in the same position as if, without any change
in the price of this commodity,
their incomes had been re-
duced by $\quad\quad\quad\quad\quad\quad\quad\quad (p_a' - p_a)\Delta$

Subtracting this last amount
from the former, we have for
remainder $\quad\quad\quad \overline{p_a'(D_a' - \Delta) - p_a(D_a - \Delta)}$

(4) $\quad\quad\quad\quad\quad\quad\quad = p_a'E - p_a(D_a - \Delta)$;

and consequently, according to our fundamental principles,
this expression will be that of the actual increase of the
national income. We have $p_a' > p_a$, and, on the other
hand, $E > D_a - \Delta$; therefore this increase is always positive and can never turn into a real decrease.

The increase would be exactly $p_a'E$, or the value exported, if exportation had not increased the price of the
commodity, and had not reduced the consumption in the

home market. This may happen with manufactured articles, and in this case the real increase would be indistinguishable from the nominal increase.

In deducing the real increase in income due to exportation of commodity M, we have not considered the loss experienced by that class of home consumers who stop buying the dearer commodity, and who thus make a use less to their liking of a part of their incomes. This loss, as has been explained, is not capable of measurement, and does not directly affect the national wealth in the commercial and mathematical sense of this term. No doubt it may affect it indirectly, if want of the dearer commodity hinders production of some other commodity, of which it is one of the raw materials ; but for the simplification and general applicability of theory, it is proper to eliminate this secondary effect to begin with, reserving for it such attention as it deserves, when we pass on to applications and to particular cases.

Moreover, by a direct and very simple method we can find this expression (4), which has just been given as that for the real increase of the national revenue due to the exportation of commodity M.

This exportation has placed market A in the enjoyment of commodities of foreign origin, of which the value is $p_a'E$. In exchange it has dispossessed it of the quantity $D_a - \Delta$ of commodity M, of which the value was $p_a(D_a - \Delta)$; the profit is $p_a'E - p_a(D_a - \Delta)$.

As to the increase in value acquired by the quantity of commodity M which continues to be consumed at A, if any *advantage* results from it to the producers of that market, this advantage will be exactly balanced by the loss experienced by consumers of the same market, so that expression (4) remains as the measure of the real value of the increase in the income of the exporting country.

89. Let us pass on to the effects of shipment of the commodity on the importing market B. The producers of commodity M on this market will experience a decrease in income expressed by $p_b D_b - p_b' D_b'$. We shall have $p_b > p_b'$, $D_b > D_b'$, and *a fortiori* $p_b D_b > p_b' D_b'$.

The consumers who were buying before the fall will transfer to the demand for other commodities R, S, T, etc., a value equal to $(p_b - p_b')D_b \quad (5)$ while consumers, whom the reduction induces to buy, will withdraw from the portion of their incomes devoted to the demand for those commodities a value $p_b'(D_b' + E - D_b) \quad (6)$

Finally, since an equivalent of the value $p_b'E$ must be withdrawn from market B in some form or other of commodity, it should be considered that a foreign sum amounting to $p_b'E \quad (7)$ is added to the funds previously devoted to the demand for commodities R, S, T, etc., other than M, in the market at B. Now, if we add quantities (5) and (7), and from their sum subtract quantity (6), we shall find for result $p_b D_b - p_b' D_b'$, a value precisely equal to that by which the incomes of the producers of commodity M in market B has been decreased. Therefore, unless it is necessary to repeat a demonstration of which the principle should have been understood, it will be recognized that this same value $p_b D_b - p_b' D_b'$ expresses at the same time the nominal diminution of the national income of B, resulting from importation of commodity M from A to B.

It must be observed that in reality the consumers, who were buying before the fall, are in exactly the same condition, after the decrease, as if their incomes had risen by the value $(p_b - p_b') D_b$

Taking the difference, we find the expression $\overline{p_b'(D_b - D_b')}$ (8)

which is that for the actual decrease of the national income of B, owing to the importation.

We do not consider, as an amount to be deducted from this actual diminution of income, the advantage resulting to consumers, who buy as a consequence of the reduction, from their thus being able to use a part of their incomes more to their liking. This advantage is incapable of valuation, and can only increase the mass of wealth indirectly, in case the article which falls in price is the raw material or the instrument for further products, a condition which must be independently considered for each particular application.

Moreover, direct considerations bring us again to expression (8), which we have given as that for the decrease in the national income of B, in consequence of the importation of commodity *M*. In fact, market B obtains the use of the value of the imported commodity, a value expressed by $p_b'E$, but for this it parts with a precisely equal value of commodities of local origin. The quantity D_b', which was being produced and consumed in market B, and which so continues after importation, falls in value, but the resulting loss to home producers is just balanced by the advantage experienced by home consumers, who buy the commodity at a lower price. As the quantity $D_b - D_b'$ ceases to be produced at B after importation, there results for home producers a loss equal to $p_b(D_b - D_b')$; but this loss is compensated for up to the point of $(p_b - p_b')(D_b - D_b)$ by the advantage to home consumers who, in consequence of importation, are able to procure for the price p_b' the same quantity which they formerly paid p_b for. Therefore, finally, the real loss caused by importation to the national income of B is equal to $p_b'(D_b - D_b')$.

It is very essential to notice that where the question is of an *exotic* commodity, or of one for which the natural conditions of production do not exist at B, on account of the climate, the soil, or the degree of wealth or intelligence of its inhabitants, the quantities D_b and D_b' become equal to zero or insignificant. In this case the national income of B does not experience either a nominal or an actual diminution in consequence of importation, while in the exporting market there is always both a nominal and an actual increase.

90. In the preceding formulas and in the accompanying explanations, it was useless to consider the cost of transportation, including wages of the agents employed in the operations necessitated by the actual transfer, merchants' profits,

and interest on the capital employed in the business. As a general rule, the transportation business may be carried on by nations foreign to both of the markets A and B, and with foreign capital. The sum total of the expenses or of the profits of transportation, equal to $(p_b' - p_a')E$, is then a source of income for a foreign nation, and is distributed among the agents and capitalists, who coöperate to carry on the transportation. If the operation were carried out by industrial agents of A, and with capital belonging to that nation, it would be necessary to add this quantity $(p_b' - p_a')E$ to the value $p_a'D_a' - p_aD_a$ which expresses the nominal increase in the national income, which arises from the sole fact of exportation; and to expression (4), which is the actual increase. This last expression would thus become

$$p_b'E - p_a(D_a - \Delta).$$

On the other hand, if the operations of transfer were carried out by industrial agents and with capital belonging to nation B, the value $(p_b' - p_a')E$ should be subtracted from $p_bD_b - p_b'D_b'$, which expresses the nominal decrease in the national income of B, which results from the fact of importation; or from quantity (8), which expresses the real decrease of the same income. We therefore have in the same way

$$p_b'(D_b - D_b') - (p_b' - p_a')E = p_a'E - p_b'\{E - (D_b - D_b')\}.$$

We have also the two inequalities

$$p_a' < p_b' \text{ and } E < E - (D_b - D_b'),$$

whence *a fortiori*, $p_a'E < p_b'\{E - (D_b - D_b')\}$.

It is worthy of particular attention, that in consequence of these inequalities, under the present hypothesis, the wages and profits provided by the carrying on of transportation will more than compensate nation *B* for the real diminution of the national income which results from importation.

On this follows the far more important corollary, that a transportation business between two fractions of the same territory, if carried on, as is usually the case, by industrial agents and by capital, both belonging to the country, necessarily increases the real value of the national income ; for this increase in income is expressed by the formula,

$$\{ p_a' E - p_a (D_a - \Delta) \} + \{ p_b' [E - (D_b - D_b')] - p_a' E \},$$

of which both of the two principal parts into which the large brackets divide the formula must necessarily be positive, according to what we have seen. This formula can be further simplified and reduced to

$$(9) \qquad p_b' \{ E - (D_b - D_b') \} - p_a (D_a - \Delta).$$

Thus it may happen that the free passage of a commodity from one part of a country to another, as we have seen in Chapter X, may fail to increase or may even diminish the total quantity produced ; it may fail to increase or may even diminish the nominal value of the national income ; but it must necessarily increase the real value of this income, as we have determined it according to conditions which have nothing arbitrary about them, and which, on the contrary, are derived naturally, in the course of the argument, from the data of the question.

In consequence, to generalize the proposition, the highest development of communications between fractions of the same territory does not necessarily raise the nominal value of the national income to a maximum, neither does it necessarily bring about the greatest possible production or operation at the fullest capacity of the national resources; but, conditions remaining otherwise the same, it does necessarily raise the real value of the national income to a maximum, and brings about the most advantageous working.

So far as I know, this fundamental principle of political economy, though always vaguely understood, has never been demonstrated by strict reasoning or deduced from its real premises. This is shown by the fact that the school of Adam Smith, with a view to removing the barriers between nation and nation, has always argued from the incontestable increase in wealth, which has been the invariable result of removal of barriers and extension of ways of communication in the interior of any single territory; although there is a fundamental disparity between the example offered as proof and the case to which it is desired to apply it; as results from the preceding calculations and as we will shortly further explain.

Between parts of the same territory the business of transportation produces an increase of national wealth which is the more apparent when the commodities in point cannot be produced or can only be produced with difficulty on the importing market; for then the term $p_b'(D_b - D_b')$, which enters negatively into expression (9), becomes equal to o, or has a value which is very small in comparison with the *positive terms.*

91. Let us return to the case where commerce goes on between one nation and another ; and, as before, let us omit from consideration the profits of transportation which may inure to the credit of the exporting nation, or to the one which imports, or to a third nation.

Let us fix our attention solely on the variations in national income which result for market A from the fact of exportation and for market B from the fact of importation. The results have been clearly demonstrated, but there are some explanations to be added to prevent specious objections.

It will be said that it is impossible for exportation of a commodity to fail to involve importation on the exporting market of a precisely equal value ; and reciprocally, importation on a market involves exportation of an equal value. Each of the markets A and B should therefore be considered as importing and exporting at the same time, and then there is no apparent reason why the wealth of the former should be affected by the establishment of communication, in any way differently from the wealth of the latter. The formulas which we have found are therefore faulty or incomplete, and the consequences deduced from them are inexact.

Moreover (and this is the favourite argument of writers of the school of Adam Smith), it should be inferred from the asserted advantage assigned to the exporting market, and the asserted disadvantage suffered by the importing market, that a nation should so arrange as always to export and never to import, which is evidently absurd, as it can only export on condition of importing, and even the sum of the values exported, calculated at the moment of leaving the

M

national market, must necessarily be equal to the sum of the values imported, calculated at the moment of arrival on the national market.

All this argumentation disappears before a few considerations, which are abstract to be sure, but which are essentially related to this subject.

If we should imagine two markets, perfectly isolated at first, and between which the barriers should be suddenly removed, it would probably happen that the removal of the barriers, by causing exportation of certain commodities M, N, P, . . . from A to B, would cause the exportation of certain commodities of a different kind R, S, T, . . . from B to A. In order, then, to appreciate the effect of removal of the barriers on the national income of A and on the national income of B, it would be necessary to consider each of these nations as acting simultaneously the part of an importing nation and that of an exporting nation, which would greatly complicate the question and lead to a complex result.

The hypothesis which we have been discussing hitherto was not of this kind ; our supposition was that there was no change in the facility of communications between markets A and B, except with reference to commodity M. It might have been assumed, in fact, that M was the only commodity of which exportation was prohibited, and that the prohibition had just been removed. What will be the effect of this removal of barriers which affects only a single commodity?

Doubtless the quantity E of commodity M cannot pass from A to B, without having an equal value imported, *directly or* in some roundabout way, from B to A ; but we have considered this foreign demand which the act of importation necessitates on market B, and we have shown that this increase in the foreign demand was more than offset by the impoverishment of the home producers of commodity M in consequence of importation, and by the reduction of the total fund which home consumers could apply to the collective demand for commodities R, S, T, ... other than M. We have likewise considered the withdrawal of a portion of the funds previously devoted to the demand for home products, which occurs on market A, for the benefit of the demand for commodities of foreign origin; showing that this diversion to the account of foreign countries was more than offset by the gain in wealth of home producers of commodity M in consequence of exportation, and by the increase in the total sum which home consumers could apply to the demand for commodities N, P, Q ... other than M. We have therefore accounted for all the data of the problem; and as, according to these data, markets A and B are not placed under symmetrical conditions, it is not surprising that we find formulas for the two markets which are unsymmetrical, and which even give results of opposite tendencies.

In consequence, absurd as it would be for a nation to export continually without ever importing; contradictory in terms as this attempt would be, since an equivalent of the value exported is always imported, whether in precious metals or otherwise, and the form is of no importance in this respect; nevertheless this theory explains the action of a government, which, in a given system of communications and business relations, raises a barrier against exportation, or opposes one to importation of a certain commodity.

The question would no longer be the same if establishment of a barrier for the benefit of *A* producers might provoke, by way of retaliation, the establishment of another barrier for the benefit of *B* producers, against whom the first barrier was raised. The government of *A* would then have to weigh the advantage resulting from the first measure to the citizens of *A* against the drawbacks caused by the retaliation. The two markets *A* and *B* would thus again be placed in symmetrical conditions, and each should be considered as acting the double part of an exporting and importing market.

92. It is evident that in all these discussions no attention has been paid for a single moment to the peculiar rôle of the monetary metals ; and the theory would be the same if the use of money did not exist, because the rôle of money is an accidental phenomenon in the theory of wealth. We will not review what has been so thoroughly developed on this point and in so many forms by Smith and writers of his school. The object of this essay is rather to present a few new views than to arrange truths already sufficiently known. By an admirable piece of dialectics full of vigour and flexibility, Smith utterly ruined the system known as *the balance of trade,* which can no longer be sustained. His own error, which was pushed much further by his disciples, was to identify with this system the theory of barriers, which does not depend on it in any way ; and this error arose naturally because the parties interested in maintaining the barriers *were* compelled to entrench themselves behind the system

which was credited at that time, and this was that of the balance of trade.

All the objections which Smith raises, not against the system of the balance of trade, but against the theory of barriers as related to the national wealth, find an answer in the principles which we have discussed. We will quote a comparison which has become a kind of a classic among his disciples. " By means of glasses, hot-beds, and hot-walls, very good grapes can be raised in Scotland, and very good wine, too, can be made of them." Therefore he suggests, according to the theory of barriers, to encourage the production of wine in Scotland, and to raise the rate of its national income, importation of French and Portuguese wines ought to be prohibited.

The answer is that wine thus produced in Scotland, supposing it to be drinkable, would be held at so high a price that there would be no demand for it, or practically none. We should, therefore, fall into the case developed in Article 89, where importation of the foreign commodity does not affect the national income at all. By prohibiting foreign wines, Scotland would deprive itself gratuitously of the enjoyments connected with the consumption of these wines. It would even deprive itself of an appreciable profit, inasmuch as Scotch industry and capital participate in the commercial circulation which brings French and Portuguese wines to the Scotch market. The case would be more complicated if importation of foreign wines caused a considerable diminution in the consumption of other spirits of home production, such as the Scotch use ; but it is probable that, on account of the high price of wine in Scotland, which is so high as to confine its use to the wealthy classes of society, the demand and the price of spirits of home production do not experience any very sensible reduction owing to importation of these wines.

93. It is further objected that when a commodity ceases to be produced in a given territory, in consequence of importation, or is only produced in smaller quantities, the raw materials of this commodity, the capital engaged in its production, and the hands employed in its manufacture, find other employment ; and that, reciprocally, when exportation encourages production of a commodity, the increase in production cannot occur without diverting hands, capital, and raw materials from other uses. But by only a casual glance at this discussion, it appears that we are arguing as if the reduction in the production of commodity M would involve suppression of the income of all those who coöperated, either by furnishing raw materials or otherwise, in the preparation of the commodity of which production ceases ; or as if increase in the production of this same commodity M, created out of whole cloth an increase for all those who contribute by furnishing raw materials or otherwise, in the preparation of the commodity now newly produced.

We have replied to this objection in advance, by the explanations given in Article 86, and we have shown how this circumstance of substitution of employment has been implicitly considered, — a very important matter, doubtless, for the producers immediately concerned, and even for society at large, in the sense that it renders less painful the transition from one commercial policy to another, but a matter *of entire* indifference when there is only under consideration the mathematical appreciation of the influence of the change in policy on the social income, after the suffering insepa- rable from a state of transition has been eliminated.

94. Let us borrow another example from a celebrated author of the school of Adam Smith, to show more plainly the disparity between our principles and the theoretical error which we are opposing. " The transportation of hemp from Riga to Havre," says J. B. Say,* "costs a Dutch ship- owner thirty-five francs a ton. No one else could do it so cheaply; but I assume that the Dutchman can. He pro- poses to the French government, which is a consumer of Russian hemp, to take charge of this transportation for forty francs a ton. He thus evidently reserves a profit of five francs. I further suppose that the French government, from a desire to favour French ship-brokers, prefers to employ French vessels, in which the same transportation will cost fifty francs, and which would have to charge fifty- five francs to provide the same profit. What will happen? The government will have spent fifteen francs a ton to pro- vide a profit of five for its citizens; and as it is the citizens who also pay the taxes, from which the public expenses are met, this operation will have cost Frenchmen fifteen francs to provide a profit of five francs for other Frenchmen."

This reasoning would be unanswerable if the French ship- broker should charter a foreign vessel, for instance an American ship, manned by American seamen, and victualled with American supplies, to go to Riga for Russian hemp to carry to Havre; in fact, then, to provide a profit of five francs a ton for the French ship-broker, or to increase the

* *Traité d'Économie Politique*, Book 1, Chapter 9

national income by the income which this profit would annually furnish the French ship-broker, the country would dispossess itself, in some form or other, for the benefit of foreign workmen and producers, of a sum of fifteen francs a ton, over and above what it would have dispossessed itself of by employing the Dutch ship-broker and the Dutch crew instead of taking the French ship-broker and the American crew.

But the loss which such a combination would cost the country is too evident for this to be what Say proposed to discuss. On the contrary, he expressly admits that the French broker employs crews of his own nationality; that the hull and tackle of his vessels are of French manufacture; that their provisions are articles of home production; and, starting from this hypothesis, he reasons as if the national income had only been increased to the extent of the broker's profits by the operation under consideration.

But of the fifty-five francs per ton which are to be divided between various French manufacturers and producers, why should the part of the broker be picked out rather than those of the captain, of the mate, of the steersman, or of the sailors who make up the crew? Or again than those of the carpenter or the rope-maker who worked on the building and tackle of the vessel in French shipyards; or rather than those of the French landlords whose products were used in the equipment and victualling of the ship? Where is the essential characteristic which distinguishes the business of the broker and the interest on his capital from the business of other agents and the return from other investments, which coöperate in the same enterprise?

This difference can only be explained by tacitly suppos-

OF THE THEORY OF WEALTH

ing that the French ship-broker would be unable to find
employment either for his skill or his capital, in case the
government should award the freight to the Dutch broker
for forty francs ; and by supposing, on the other hand, that
the members of the crew would find employment on other
vessels, or that other trades would offer them equivalent
wages ; by making a similar supposition for the ship-
builders ; and, finally, by admitting that other outlets would
be found for the commodities which entered into the construction, the gear, and victualling of the French vessels
which the government ceases to charter.

But the supposition made concerning the ship-broker is
quite as gratuitous as the opposite supposition, which concerns the other home producers or agents ; and, moreover,
this circumstance that for certain agents or producers, other
employments and other outlets may be substituted for the
employment and outlet which are cut off, — this circumstance, we say, really has nothing to do with the question.
France dispossesses itself, in one form or another, of the
value of forty francs per ton to pay the Dutch charter. This
value stops providing the income of certain French workmen
and producers. If as many vessels are to continue to be
built, equipped, and victualled, it will be necessary for funds
to be diverted, up to due competition, from other demands.
The loss will be thrown back on other classes of workmen
and producers, but the fall in the national income will be
the same, with reservation always of the reactions and perturbations *of the second order*, which are too involved for
general consideration.

Under the present hypothesis, the government will have

two things to consider, for it evidently cannot prefer its own citizens to foreigners *at any price*, unless interest in the public safety enters into the question, as, for instance (as J. B. Say very well observes), if encouragement of merchant shipping were indispensable to the maintenance of the navy, which itself could not be abandoned without detriment to security and political power of the State. Except for this major consideration, which is beyond our province, the administration will have to consider whether the encouragement given to national merchant shipping is not excessive : (1) because it consumes commodities and services which might be used in a more remunerative way, *i.e.* more usefully for an ultimate increase of the national wealth ; (2) because it unjustly burdens the public treasury, *i.e.* the citizens at large, in order to increase the income of certain special classes of producers ; for it is not enough that the national income increases, and that thus these gain more than the others lose : the principles of equity which belong to all countries and all times ; the principles of equity which more particularly rule the country and the time in which we live, do not permit that acts of the public authority should have for their tendency to increase the natural inequality of conditions.

95. We have just laid a finger on the question which is at the bottom of all discussions on measures which prohibit or restrict freedom of trade. It is not enough to accurately analyze the influence of such measures on the national income ; their tendency as to the distribution of the wealth of society should also be looked into. We have no intention of taking up here this delicate question, which would *carry us too* far away from the purely abstract discussions

with which this essay has to do. If we have tried to overthrow the doctrine of Smith's school as to barriers, it was only from theoretical considerations, and not in the least to make ourselves the advocates of prohibitory and restrictive laws. Moreover, it must be recognized that such questions as that of commercial liberty are not settled either by the arguments of scientific men or even by the wisdom of statesmen. A higher power drives nations in this direction or that, and when the day of a system is past, good reasons cannot restore its lost vitality any more than sophisms. The skill of statesmen, then, consists in tempering the ardour of the spirit of innovation, without attempting an impossible struggle against the laws of Providence. Possession of a sound theory may help in this labour of resistance to abrupt changes and assist in easing the transition from one system to another. By giving more light on a debated point, it soothes the passions which are aroused. Systems have their fanatics, but the science which succeeds to systems never has them. Finally, even if theories relating to social organization do not guide the doings of the day, they at least throw light on the history of accomplished facts. Up to a certain point it is possible to compare the influence of economic theories on society to that of grammarians on language. Languages are formed without the consent of grammarians, and are corrupted in spite of them; but their works throw light on the laws of the formation and decadence of languages; and their rules hasten the time when a language attains its perfection, and delay a little the invasions of barbarism and bad taste which corrupt it.

BIBLIOGRAPHY

OF

MATHEMATICAL ECONOMICS

———◆◆◆———

FROM CEVA TO COURNOT

(1711–1837)

1711 CEVA, Giovanni. De re nummaria, quoad fieri potuit geometrice tractata, ad illustrissimos et excellentissimos dominos Praesidem Quaestoresque hujus arciducalis Caesaraei Magistratus Mantuae. Mantova, 4°, 60 pp. [Reviewed by F. Nicolini, *Giorn. degli econ.*, Oct. 1878. See also Palgrave's Dict.]

1717 MARIOTTE, Esme. Essaie de logique. 2d ed. In collected works. Leide. [See Principe 97 and 11me partie, art. III.] -

1738 BERNOUILLI, Daniel. Specimen theoriae novae de mensura sortis. *Commentarii academiae scientiarum imperialis Petropolitanae*, vol. V, pp. 175–92. [German transl., 1896, by A. Pringsheim: Die Grundlage der modernen Wertlehre. Versuch einer neuen Theorie der Wertbestimmung von

173

Glücksfällen (Einleitung von Ludwig Fick). Leipzig (Duncker & Humblot), 60 pp.]

1754 ANON. [F. Forbonnais]. Élémens du commerce, 2d ed., vol. II, chs. viii, ix, Leyde & Paris, 12°.

1764 BECCARIA, Cesare. Tentativo analitico sui contrabbandi, 1764–5. Estratto dal foglio periodico intitolato : *Il caffè*, vol. I, Brescia. [Also in Custodi's Scrittori classici Italiani di economia politica, parte moderna, vol. XII, pp. 235–41, Milano, 1804.]

1771 ANON. [probably Maj. Gen. Henry Lloyd]. An essay on the theory of money. London, 161 pp.

1781 ANON. [A. N. Isnard]. Traité des richesses. London & Lausanne, 2 vols., xxiv, 344, 327 pp. [Slightly math.]

1786 ANON. [Condorcet]. Vie de M. Turgot, pp. 162–9, London. [Eng. transl., 1787, pp. 403–9.]

1792 SILIO, Guglielmo. Saggio sull' influenza dell' analisi nelle scienze politiche ed economiche. Nuova raccolta d' opuscoli di autori Siciliani, vol. V (?), Palermo.

1801 CANARD, N. F. Principes d'économie politique, ouvrage couronné par l'Institut. Paris (Buisson), 235 pp. [Reviewed by Francis Horner, *Edinburgh Rev.*, no. II.]

1802 KRÖNCKE, Claus. Versuch einer Theorie des Fuhrwerks mit Anwendung auf den Strassenbau. Giessen.

1803 SIMONDE, J. C. L. De la richesse commerciale, vol. I, pp. 105–9, Geneva.

1804 KRÖNCKE, Claus. Das Steuerwesen nach seiner Natur und seinen Wirkungen untersucht. Darmstadt & Giessen (Heyer), xxxii, 440 pp.

1809   LANG, Joseph. Ueber den obersten Grundsatz der politischen Oekonomie. Riga.

1810   KRÖNCKE, Claus. Anleitung zur Regulirung der Steuer.

1811   LANG, Joseph. Grundlinien der politischen Arithmetik. Kursk (Langner), xxii, 216 pp.

1815   BUQUOY, Georg von. Die Theorie der Nationalwirthschaft, nach einem neuen Plane und nach mehreren eigenen Ansichten dargestellt. Leipzig, 4°. [3 Nachträge : 1816, 1817 (524 pp.), 1818.]

1816   ANON. [L. M. Valeriani]. Apologia della formola $p = \dfrac{i}{o}$, trattandosi del come si determini il prezzo delle cose tutte mercatabili, contro ciò che ne dice il celebre autore del "Nuova prospetto delle scienze economiche." Bologna (Marsigli), 62 pp.

1817   ANON. [L. M. Valeriani]. Discorso apologetico in cui si sostiene recarsi invano pel celebre autore del "Nuovo prospetto delle scienze economiche" contro l' Apologia della formola $p = \dfrac{i}{o}$ trattando si del come si determini il prezzo delle cose tutte mercatabili, ciò che il medisimo ha scritto nel tomo II, il pag. 114–117, 141–146, e nel IV, pag. 214–219, 244–263 dell' opera suddetta. Bologna (Marsigli), 114 pp.

1824   ANON. [T. Perronet Thompson]. The instrument of exchange. *Westminster Rev.*, vol. I, pp. 171–205. [Reprinted separately, 1830, 27 pp. ; postscript to same, *Westmin. Rev.*, 1830, vol. XII, pp. 525–33 ; reprinted 1842 in : Exercises, political and others, vol. III, pp 295–343.]

1825   CAZAUX, L. F. G. de.   Elémens d'économie privée et
       publique. Paris (Huzard) & Toulouse (Doula-
       doure), 251 pp. [Slightly math.]
1825   FUCCO, Francesco.   Saggi economici, 1st ser., vol. 2.
       Pisa, 1825–27. [Math.?]
1826   RAU, K. H.   Grundsätze der Volkswirthschaftslehre.
       [Subsequent editions, 1833, '37, '41, '63, '68,
       Leipzig & Heidelberg. Very slightly math.]
1826   THOMPSON, T. Perronet.   On rent.
1826   THÜNEN, J. H. von.   Der isolirte Staat in Beziehung
       auf Landwirthschaft und Nationalökonomie, oder
       Untersuchungen über den Einfluss, den die Ge-
       treidepreise, der Reichthum des Bodens und die
       Abgaben auf den Ackerbau ausüben.   1er Th.,
       Hamburg, viii, 290 pp. [2d ed. of same, 1842,
       Rostock, xv, 391 pp. ; 1er fasc. von 2ter Th., 1850,
       Rostock, vi, 285 pp. ; 2ter fasc. von 2ter Th., 1863,
       Rostock, ix, 444 pp. French transl. by Leverrière,
       1851, Paris (Guillaumin), viii, 340 pp. ; French
       transl. by Wolkoff (of fasc. of 1850), 1857, Paris.
       Slightly math.]
1829   WHEWELL, William.   Mathematical exposition of
       some doctrines of political economy. *Cambridge
       Philos. Trans.*, vol. III, pp. 191–230, 4° [Con-
       tinued, 1831, vol. IV, pp. 155–98 ; 1850, vol. IX,
       pp. 128–49, and Part II, pp. [1–7] ; Italian transl.
       in *Biblioteca dell' econ.*, 1875, 3d ser., vol. II, pp.
       1–65.]
1832   LUBÉ, D. G.   Argument against the gold standard.
       London, iv, 192 pp.

FROM COURNOT TO JEVONS

(1838–1870)

GENERAL TREATISES

1838 COURNOT, Augustin. Recherches sur les principes mathématiques de la théorie des richesses. Paris (Hachette), xi, 198 pp. [Italian transl. in *Biblioteca dell' econ.*, 1875, 3d ser., vol. II, pp. 67–170. English transl., by N. T. Bacon, in : Economic classics, New York & London (Macmillan), 1897.]

1844 HAGEN, K. H. System of political economy. Transl. from German by J. P. Smith. London, viii, 88 pp.

1848 MILL, J. S. Principles of political economy. [Bk. III, ch. xviii, § 7, very slightly math.]

1849 ESMÉNARD DU MAZET, Camille. Nouveaux principes d'économie politique. Paris (Joubert), ix, 456 pp.

1849 WOLKOFF, Mathieu. ,Prémisses philosophiques de l'économie rationelle des sociétés. Paris (Guillaumin). [2d ed., 1861 : Lectures d'économie politique rationelle, 12°, 309 pp. ; 3d ed., 1868 : Précis d'écon. pol. rat. (math. notes, pp. 293–5 ; 308–12).]

1854 GOSSEN, H. H. Entwickelung der Gesetze des menschlichen Verkehrs, und der daraus fliessenden Regeln für menschliches Handeln. Braunschweig, 278 pp. [Reviewed by Hooper, *Jour. Roy. Statist. Soc.*, 1879, pp. 729–33 ; by Walras, *Jour. des econ.*, 1885, 4th ser., vol. XXX, pp. 68–90. See also preface to Jevons's Theory Pol. Econ., 1879, '88, and Palgrave's Dictionary. Republished, 1888, Berlin (Prager).]
N

1855   JENNINGS, Richard. Natural elements of political economy. London, 275 pp. [Math.?]

1856   BENNER. Théorie mathématique de l'économie politique.

1858   COURCELLE SENEUIL, J. G. Traité théorique et pratique d'économie politique. Paris (Amyot). [2d ed., 1867, viii, 495, 538 pp. X. Very slightly math.]

1860   DU MESNIL-MARIGNY, J. Les libre échangistes et les protectionnistes conciliés, ou solution complète des principales questions économiques. Paris (Guillaumin). [2d ed., 1860, ii, 413 pp.; 3d ed., 1878.]

1863   DU MESNIL-MARIGNY, J. Catéchisme de l'économie politique. Paris (Guillaumin), 12°, 355 pp. [Math. notes.]

1863   MANGOLDT, H. von. Grundriss der Volkswirthschaftslehre. Stuttgart (Engelhorn), xvi, 224 pp.

ON VALUE, TAXATION, AND DISTRIBUTION

1838   TOZER, John. Mathematical investigation of the effect of machinery on the wealth of a community in which it is employed, and on the fund for the payment of wages. *Cambridge Philos. Trans.*, vol. VI, pp. 507–22, 4°. [Continued under title: On the effect of the non-residence of landlords, etc., *ibid.*, 1840, vol. VII, pp. 189–96.]

1844   DUPUIT, E. J. De la mesure de l'utilité des travaux publics. *Annales des ponts et chaussées*, 2d ser., vol. VIII, pp. 332–75, Paris.

1849   DUPUIT, E. J. De l'influence des péages sur l'utilité des voies de communication. *Annales des ponts et chaussées*, 2d ser., no. 207, pp. 170–248, Paris.

1851 ESMÉNARD DU MAZET, Camille. De la valeur comme première notion de l'économie politique. Paris (Joubert), 23 pp. [Slightly math.]

1853 FARR, William. Income and property tax. *Jour. Roy. Statist. Soc.*, vol. XVI, pp. 3–44.

1853 HARDY, Peter. An *exposé* of the fallacy "that it is just to tax temporary annuities at the same rate as perpetual annuities." *Assur. Mag. and Jour. Inst. Actuaries*, vol. III, pp. 195–204.

1853 JELLICOE, Charles. On the true measure of liability in a system of direct taxation. *Assur. Mag. and Jour. Inst. Actuaries*, vol. III, pp. 1–7.

1856 WOLKOFF, Mathieu. Le salaire naturel d'après M. de Thünen. *Jour. des écon.*, 2d ser., vol. X, pp. 263–70.

1857 WOLKOFF, Mathieu. Nouvelles observations au sujet de l'ouvrage de M. de Thünen sur le salaire naturel. *Jour. des écon.*, 2d ser., vol. XVI.

1859 BOCCARDO, Gerolamo. Lavori pubblici. Dizion. econ. polit. e commer., vol. II, pp. 652–3, Torino, 4°.

1864 FAUVEAU, G. Considérations mathématiques sur la théorie de l'impôt. Paris, 64 pp.

1865 KNAPP, G. F. Zur Prüfung der Untersuchungen Thünen's über Lohn und Zinsfuss im isolirten Staate. Braunschweig, 35 pp.

1867 BRENTANO, L. J. Ueber J. H. von Thünen's naturgemässen Lohn und Zinsfuss im isolirten Staate. [Inaugural dissertation. Göttingen, 59 pp.; pp. 48–59 math.]

1867 FAUVEAU, G. Considérations mathématiques sur la

théorie de la valeur. *Jour. des écon.*, 3d ser., vol. V, pp. 31–40.

1868 JENKIN, Fleeming. The graphic representation of the laws of supply and demand and their application to labour. [Reprinted in Grant's Recess studies, 1870. pp. 151–85. Edinburgh. Also in Papers of Fleeming Jenkin, London, 1887, vol. II, pp. 76–107.]

1868 MARX, Karl. Das Kapital. Kritik der politischen Oekonomie. Hamburg (Meissner), vol. I, xxvii, 526 pp. [2d ed., 1873 ; 3d ed. (ed. by F. Engels), 1883 ; vol. II (Engels), 1885 ; vol. III (Engels), 1894 ; vol. I, transl. into Russian, 1872 ; into French, by M. J. Roy, Paris (Lachâtre), and revised by author, 1873 ; into English from 3d German ed. by S. Moore and E. Aveling, and ed. by F. Engels, 1886 : reprinted in Humboldt libr. sci., New York, 1891. Very slightly math.]

1869 SCHUMACHER, H. Ueber J. H. von Thünen's Gesetz vom naturgemässen Arbeitslohne. Rostock, 84 pp.

MISCELLANEOUS

1839 ELLET, C. An essay on the laws of trade in reference to the works of internal improvement in the United States, viii, 248 pp.

1840 ANON. [J. W. Lubbock]. On currency. London (Knight), viii, 43, xxi pp.

1844 HAGEN, K. H. Die Nothwendigkeit der Handelsfreiheit für das Nationaleinkommen, mathematisch nachgewiesen. Königsberg (Gräfe & Unger), 32 pp.

1850 LARDNER, Dionysius. Railway economy. London. [Chapters xii and xiii math.]

1852 JELLICOE, Charles. On the contrivances required to render contingent reversionary interests marketable securities. *Assur. Mag.*, vol. II, pp. 159–66.

1854 WOLKOFF, Mathieu. Opuscules sur la rente foncière. Paris, 231 pp.

1856 JELLICOE, Charles. The bank of England : its present constitution and operation. *Jour. Roy. Statist. Soc.*, vol. XIX, pp. 272–83. [Very slightly math.]

1859 VAN HOUTEN, S. Verhandeling over de Waarde.

1863 MACLEOD, H. D. Credit. MacLeod's Dictionary of pol. econ., pp. 567–617. [Very slightly math.]

1866 JEVONS, W. S. Brief account of a general mathematical theory of political economy. *Jour. Roy. Statist. Soc.*, vol. XXIX, pp. 282–3.

1867 WITTSTEIN, Theodor. Mathematische Statistik und deren Anwendung auf National-Ökonomie und Versicherungs-Wissenschaft. Hannover (Hahn'sche Hofbuchh.), 55 pp.

1868 GRAY, Peter. On rate of interest in loans repayable per instalments. *Jour. Inst. Actuaries*, pp. 91–102, 182–9.

1868 JENKIN, Fleeming. Trades Unions. How far legitimate. *North Brit. Rev.*, Mar. [Footnote math.]

1870 LEFÈVRE, H. Traité théorique et pratique des valeurs mobilières et des opérations de bourse. Paris (Lachaud).

1870 LEFÈVRE, H. Théorie élémentaire des opérations de bourse.

FROM JEVONS TO MARSHALL

(1871-1889)

GENERAL TREATISES

1871   JEVONS, W. Stanley. The theory of political economy.
London (Macmillan), xvi, 267 pp. [2d ed., 1879 ;
3d ed., 1888, lii, 296 pp.   Italian transl., 1875,
in *Biblioteca dell' econ.*, Torino, 3d ser., vol. II,
pp. 4174-4311.]

1874   WALRAS, Léon. Éléments d'économie politique pure,
ou théorie de la richesse sociale.   1st fasc., Lausanne, Paris & Bâle, viji, 208 pp. [2d fasc., 1877,
pp. 209-407 ; 2d ed., 1889, xxiv, 524 pp. ; 3d
ed., 1896, xxiv, 495 pp.   The 3d ed. contains the
2d, 3d, 4th, and 5th essays in the list cited below
under : Théorie math. de la rich. soc. 1883 ; also
reprints of : Théorème de l'utilité maxima des
capitaux neufs. *Rev. d'écon. pol.*, vol. III, 1889,
pp. 310-15 ; Observations sur le principe de la
théorie du prix de MM. Auspitz et Lieben, *ibid.*,
1890, May-June. [Answered by Messrs. A. & L.,
ibid., 1890, p. 599.] ; De l'échange de plusieurs
marchandises entre elles. *Bull. soc. ingen. civils.*
Jan., 1891 [Eng. transl., Ann. Amer. Acad.,
Jul., '92.] ; Théorie géométrique de la détermi-
nation des prix.   (Rec. inaug. de l'univ. de
Lausanne.) [Eng. transl., *ibid.*] ; Note sur la re-
futation de la théorie anglais du fermage de M.
Wicksteed. *Recueil publ. par l'Univ. de Lausanne*, 1896.]

1879 MARSHALL, Alfred & Mary P. The economics of industry. London, xiv, 231 pp. [Slightly math.]

1881 MACLEOD, H. D. The elements of economics. London (Longmans), vol. I. [vol. II, part I, 1886 ; slightly math.]

1881 SACHER, Eduard. Grundzüge einer Mechanic der Gesellschaft, I. Theoretischer Theil. Jena (Fischer), 246 pp.

1883 WALRAS, Léon. Théorie mathématique de la richesse sociale. Lausanne, 4°, 256 pp. [Reproduction of: Principe d'une théorie mathématique de l'échange. Orléans (Colas), 1873, 24 pp. (reprinted *Jour. des écon.*, June, 1874, pp. 5-21) : Equations de l'échange. Lausanne, 1875 ; Equations de la production. Lausanne, 1876 ; Equations de la capitalisation, 1876, 40 pp. ; Théorie mathématique du bimetallisme. Paris, 1876, '81, '82, *Jour. des écon;* Théorie mathématique du billet de banque, 1879. *Bull. soc. vaudoise sci. nat.;* Théorie mathématique du prix des terres et de leur rachat par l'état, 1880. *Bull. soc. vaudoise sci. nat.* The first four have been translated into Italian and German, viz. : in *Biblioteca econ.*, 1878, 3d ser., vol. II, pp. 1289-1388, and as Math. Theorie der Preisbestimmung, Stuttgart (Enke), 1881.]

1884 PIERSON, N. G. Leerboek der staathuishoudkunde. Erste deel. Haarlem. [Part II, 1890 ; 2d ed. of Part I, 1896, 671 pp.; part II, 1897. Very slightly math.]

1885 LAUNHARDT, Wilhelm. Mathematische Begründung der Volkswirtschaftslehre. Leipzig, viii, 216 pp.

1886 NEWCOMB, Simon. Principles of political economy.
New York, xvi, 543 pp. [Slightly math.]

1887 VAN DORSTEN, R. K. Mathematische onderzoekin-
gen op het gebied der staathuishoudkunde. Ar
chief voor politieke en sociale rekenkunde. 1 deel,
3de en 4de aflevering.

1887 WESTERGAARD, Harald. Mathematiken i National-
ökonomiens Tjeneste. In volume : Smaaskrifte
tilegnede A. F. Krieger. Copenhagen.

1888 WICKSTEED, Philip H. The alphabet of economic
science. I, Elements of the theory of value or
worth. London, xv, 142 pp., 12°.

1889 EFFERTZ, Otto. Arbeit und Boden. Bd. I, Berlin
(Puttkammer & Mühlbrecht). [2d ed., 1890,
xxii, 348 pp. Bde. II, III, 1891, xxxi, 304 and
xxiv, 127 pp.]

ON VALUE, TAXATION, AND DISTRIBUTION

Value

1873 WALRAS, Léon. Abstract of ' Principe d'une théorie
mathématique d'échange' [see 'General Treatises,'
1883]. *Bull. soc. vaudoise des sci. nat.* Lausanne,
vol. XII, pp. 317-21.

1874 ZANON, G. A. Sulla teoria matematica dello scambio
del professore M. L. Walras, lettera al professore
Alberto Errera. Estratto dalla Rassegna di agri-
coltura, industria, e commercio. Padova, 7 pp.

1875 FONTANEAU, E. De la valeur. *Jour. actuaires
français*, vol. IV, pp. 175-99, 267-77.

1876 WESTERGAARD, Harald. Den moralske Formue og
det moralske Haab. *Tidsskrift for Math.*

1876 ZAMBELLI, Andrea. La teoria matematica dello scambio del Signor Leone Walras. Lettera diretta al professore Errera dott. Alberto. Padova, 28 pp.

1877 MOLL, C. L. Der Werth. Eine neue Theorie desselben. Leipzig (Felix), 48 pp.

1879 MARSHALL, Alfred. The pure theory of (domestic) values. Cambridge, 24 pp. [Privately printed.]

1879 MARSHALL, Alfred. The pure theory of foreign trade. Cambridge. [Privately printed.]

1884. EDGEWORTH, F. Y. The rationale of exchange. *Jour. Roy. Statist. Soc.*, vol. XLVII, pp. 164–6. [Very slightly math.]

1884 WIESER, Friedrich von. Ueber den Ursprung und die Hauptgesetze des wirthschaftlichen Werthes. Wien (Hölder), xiv, 214 pp. [Very slightly math.]

1886 ANTONELLI, G. B. Sulla teoria matematica della economia politica. Pisa, 31 pp.

1888 NICHOLSON, J. S. Article: "Value." Encycl. Brit., vol. XXIV, pp. 45–52. [Slightly math.]

1889 AUSPITZ (RUDOLF) & LIEBEN (RICHARD). Untersuchungen über die Theorie des Preises. Leipzig (Duncker & Humblot), xxxi, 555 pp. [Chapter I appeared in 1887 as: Zur Theorie des Preises, vii, 52 pp.]

1889 LEHR, Julius. Grenzwert, Grenznutzen und Preis. *Jahrb. Nationaloek. u. Statist.*

1889 LEHR, Julius. Zur Lehre vom Preise. *Vierteljahrschr. Volkswirth.* (Berlin).

1889 ROSSI, Giovanni. La matematica applicata alla teoria della ricchezza sociale. In: *Studi bibliogr. storici e critici e nuovo ricerche.* Reggio-Emilia.

1889 WIFSER, Friedrich von. Der natürliche Werth. Wien,
237 pp. [English transl. by C. A. Malloch, ed. by
W. Smart, 1893, London & New York (Macmillan),
xiv, 243 pp. Very slightly math.]

Taxation

1871 FAUVEAU, G. Rendement maximum de l'impôt indirect. *Jour. des écon.*, 3d ser., vol. XXIV, pp.
445-8.

1871 JENKIN, Fleeming. On the principles which regulate the incidence of taxes. *Proc. Roy. Soc. Edinburgh*, sess. '71-'72, pp. 618-31. [Reprinted,
1887, in Papers of Fleeming Jenkin, London, pp.
107-22.]

1875 ACHARD, A. Influence des taxes qui frappent les
obligations sur leur prix d'après un taux d'intérêt
déterminé. *Jour. des actuaires français*, vol. IV,
Jan., pp. 70-74.

1877 LEHR, Julius. Kritische Bemerkungen zu den wichti-
geren für und wider den progressiven Steuerfuss
vorgebrachten Gründen. *Jahrb. für Nationaloek.
und Statist.*

1880 SCHÄFFLER, Hermann. Ueber die Normirung der
Einkommensteuer. *Vierteljahrschr. Volkswirthsch.,
Polit. und Kulturgesch.*, 17th year, vol. IV, pp.
1-38.

1882 PANTALEONI, Maffeo. La traslazione dei tributi.
Roma (Paolini).

1887 PANTALEONI, Maffeo. Teoria della pressione tributaria e metodi per misurarla. Parte prima, teoria
della pressione tributaria. Roma, 78 pp.

1889 COHEN STUART, A. J. Bijdrage tot de theorie der progressieve inkomstenbelasting. 'S-gravenhage.

1889 MEES, A. W. De progressieve inkomstenbelasting. *Economist.*

Distribution

1873 F. BING og JULIUS PETERSEN. Bestemmelse af den rationelle Arbejdslön samt nogle Bemaerkninger om Ökonomiens Methode. *Nationaloek. Tidsskrift* (Copenhagen), vol. I, pp. 296.

1874 D'AULNIS DE BOUROUILL, Johan. Het inkomen der maatschappij. Eene proeve van theoretische staathuishoudkunde. Leiden, xiii, 215 pp.

1875 FALCK, Georg von. Die thünensche Lehre vom Bildungsgesetz des Zinsfusses und vom naturgemässen Arbeitslohn. Leipzig (Bidder), 55 pp. [pp. 18–55 math.]

1879 VAN DEN BERG, C. P. J. De theorie van het arbeidsloon. Utrecht, 35 pp. [English transl., 1880, London, 25 pp.]

1883 PANTALEONI, Maffeo. Contributo alla teoria del riparto della spese pubbliche. *La Rassegna Italiana,* year III, vol. IV, no. 1, pp. 25–60.

1884 SCHROEDER, E. A. Das Unternehmen und der Unternehmergewinn. Wien (Gerold), x, 92 pp.

1886 LEHR, J. K. Marx, Das Kapital, Kritik der politischen Oekonomie. *Vierteljahrsch. für Volkswirtsch.* Bd. XC, pp. 1–38, 97–123; Bd. XCI, pp. 34–60.

1887 GIDDINGS, F. H. The natural rate of wages. *Pol. Sci. Quart.,* vol. II, pp. 620–37. [Very slightly math.]

1887   SCHMIDT, Conrad.   Der   natürliche   Arbeitslohn.
       (Staatswiss. Studien,) Jena, 87 pp.

1887   WALKER, F. A.   The source of business profits.
       Quart. Jour. Econ., vol. I, pp. 265–88. [Very
       slightly math.]

1888   MUNRO & *others*.   Report of the committee, consist-
       ing of Professor Sidgwick, Professor Foxwell, Mr.
       A. H. D. Acland, the Rev. W. Cunningham, and
       Professor Munro (Sect.), on the regulation of
       wages by means of lists in the cotton industry.
       Rep't. Brit. Assoc. Adv. Sci. for 1887, pp. 303–20.

1889   WOOD, Stuart.   The theory of wages. *Public. Amer.
       Econ. Assoc.*, vol. IV, pp. 5–35.   [Slightly math.]

MISCELLANEOUS

Methodology

1872   MARCHAND, J.   Recherche sur la méthode à adopter
       pour la discussion des éléments de la statistique.
       Jour. des actuaires français, vol. I, pp. 267–73,
       393–409.   [Continued, 1873, vol. II, pp. 58–78,
       251–63; 1874, vol. III, pp. 307–25.]

1875   BOCCARDO, Gerolamo.   Dell' applicazione dei metodi
       quantitativi alle scienze economiche, statistiche e
       sociale.   Saggio di logica economica. *Bibl. econ.*,
       vol. II, pp. i–lxxii.   [New ed., 1878.]

1875   JEVONS, W. S.   The progress of the mathematical
       theory of political economy, with an explanation
       of the principles of the theory.   *Transactions of
       the Manchester Statist. Soc.*, pp. 1–19.

1876   WALRAS, Léon.   Un nuovo ramo della matematica.

Dell' applicazione delle matematiche all' economia
politica. *Giorn. degli econ.* (Padova), April.

1878 MANDELLO, Károly. Erkölcstan és mennyiségtan az
értékelméletben. [Ethics and mathematics in the
theory of value.] *Nemzetgazdasági szemle.* [*Econ.
Review.*] Budapest. [Very slightly math.]

1885 MARSHALL, Alfred. On the graphic method of statistics. (Read at Internat. statist. cong., June 23,
1885.) *Jour. Statist. Soc.* (London), 10 pp.

1887 HELM, Georg. Die bisherigen Versuche, Mathematik
auf volkswirthschaftliche Fragen anzuwenden.
Ges. Isis in Dresden, Abth. I, pp. 3-13.

1889 EDGEWORTH, F. Y. Points at which mathematical
reasoning is applicable to political economy.
Nature, Sept., pp. 496-509.

1889 EDGEWORTH, F. Y. On the application of mathematics to political economy. (Address of Pres.
Sect. F, Brit. Assoc., 59th meet., Newcastle-upon-
Tyne, Sept. '89.) *Jour. Roy. Statist. Soc.*, London, vol. LII, pt. I, pp. 538-76.

Money

1881 FAUVEAU, G. Comparaison du pouvoir de la monnaie
à deux époques différentes. *Jour. des écon.*, 4th
sér., vol. XIV, pp. 354-9.

1883 EDGEWORTH, F. Y. The method of ascertaining a
change in the value of gold. *Jour. Roy. Statist.
Soc.* (London), vol. XLVI, pp. 714-18.

1884 JEVONS, W. S. Investigations in currency and finance.
London (Macmillan), xliv, 428 pp. [Slightly
math.]

1885 LAUNHARDT, Wilhelm.   Das Wesen des Geldes und
        die Währungsfrage.   Leipzig (Engelmann), vi,
        75 pp.   [Very slightly math.]
1887 NICHOLSON, J. S.   The measurement of variations in
        the value of the monetary standard. *Jour. Roy.
        Statist. Soc.*, pp. 150-66.
1888 EDGEWORTH, F. Y.   Some methods of measuring
        variations in general prices. *Jour. Roy. Statist.
        Soc.*, pp. 346-68.
1888 EDGEWORTH, F. Y.   Report of the committee con-
        sisting of Mr. S. Bourne, Professor F. Y. Edge-
        worth (secretary), Professor H. S. Foxwell, Mr.
        Robert Giffen, Professor Alfred Marshall, Mr. J. B.
        Martin, Professor J. S. Nicholson, Mr. R. H. Inglis
        Palgrave, and Professor H. Sidgwick, appointed for
        the purpose of investigating the best methods of
        ascertaining and measuring variations in the value
        of the monetary standard.   Memorandum by the
        Sec. *Rep't Brit. Assoc. Adv. Sci.* for 1887, pp. 247-
        301.   [2d report, 1889, in *Rep't Brit. Assoc.* for
        1888, pp. 181-209 ; 3d report, 1890, in *Rep't Brit.
        Assoc.* for 1889, pp. 133-64.]
1888 EDGEWORTH, F. Y.   The mathematical theory of
        banking. *Jour. Roy. Statist. Soc.* (London),
        March.
1888 NICHOLSON, J. S.   A treatise on money and essays on
        monetary problems.   [2d ed., 1893, London
        (Black), 415 pp.]   [Slightly math.]
1889 EDGEWORTH, F. Y.   Appreciation of gold.   *Quart.
        Jour. Econ.*, vol. III, pp. 153-69.
1889 EDGEWORTH, F. Y.   Report of the committee con-
        sisting of Mr. S. Bourne, Professor F. Y. Edgeworth

(secretary), Professor H. S. Foxwell, Mr. Robert Giffen, Professor Alfred Marshall, Mr. J. B. Martin, Professor J. S. Nicholson, and Mr. R. H. Inglis Palgrave, appointed for the purpose of inquiring and reporting as to the statistical data available for determining the amount of the precious metals in use as money in the principal countries, the chief forms in which the money is employed, and the amount annually used in the arts. Memorandum by the secretary on Jevons's method of ascertaining the number of coins in circulation. *Rep't Brit. Assoc. Adv. Sci.* for 1888, pp. 219–32.

1889 MACLEOD, H. D. The theory of credit. Vol. I. London (Longmans), xii, 336 pp. [Very slightly math.]

Transportation

1872 LAUNHARDT, Wilhelm. Kommerzielle Trassirung der Verkehrswege. Hannover.

1873 JAŸ, Aimé. Des relations entre les chemins de fer et l'état, considérées au point de vue financier. *Jour. des actuaires français,* vol. II, pp. 173–99.

1876 MADSEN, C. L. Den sandsynlige Lov for den internationale Telegraftrafik. Copenhagen. [Continued, 1878, *Nationaloek. Tidsskrift,* Bd. XI, pp. 171–83. English : On the law of international telegraph traffic. *Jour. Soc. Telegraph Engineers,* vol. VII, pp. 198–215. London & New York.]

1877 MADSEN, C. L. Nye Undersögelser om Loven for den internationale Trafik. Foredrag i det Kge. danske geographiske Selskab. *Geografisk Tidsskrift,* Bd. I, pp. 192–201, Copenhagen, 1877.

192 BIBLIOGRAPHY OF

[French transl., 1877, Recherches sur la loi du
mouvement télégraphique international. Paris
(Dentu), ix, 68 pp., avec 10 tableaux.]

1878 C. L. MADSEN and Harald WESTERGAARD. Correspondence. *Nationaloek. Tidsskrift.*

1878 WESTERGAARD, Harald. Den sandsynlige Lov for den
internationale Telegraftrafik. *Nationaloek. Tidsskrift*, Bd. XI.

1879 LEHR, Julius. Eisenbahn-Tarifwesen und Eisenbahn-
Monopol. Berlin.

1879 MADSEN, C. L. Danmarks, Sveriges og Norges
Samkvem med Udlandet, 1871–77. Copenhagen,
4°, xxiv, 26 pp.

1883 LAUNHARDT, Wilhelm. Wirthschaftliche Fragen des
Eisenbahnwesens. *Centralblatt der Bauverwaltung.*

1885 LEHR, Julius. Wirthschaftliche Fragen des Eisenbahnwesens. *Deutsche Bauzeitung* (Berlin).

1887 LAUNHARDT, Wilhelm. Theorie des Trassirens der
Eisenbahnen. Heft I, 1887, iv, 112 pp.; Heft II,
1888. Hannover (Schmorl & Seefeld).

1887 PICARD, A. Traité des chemins de fer. 4 vols.
Paris (Rothschild). [Parts math.]

1888 HADLEY, A. T. Railroad transportation; its history
and its laws. New York & London (Putnam), v,
269 pp. [Appendix II, math., 2 pp.]

1888 AMBROZAVICS, Béla. Der gemeinschaftliche Nutzen
der Eisenbahnen und dessen Berechnung. [French
transl.: Le tarif par zones des chemins de fer
hongrois et ma théorie. Bruxelles (Weissen-
bruch), 1895. Italian transl. by Carlo Nagel,
Milano (Ingegneri), 1895.]

Unclassified

1872 MARCHAND, J.   Recherche sur la méthode à adopter
pour la discussion des éléments de la statistique.
Jour. des actuaires français, vol. I, pp. 267–73,
393–409, Paris. [Continued, vol. II, pp. 58–78,
251–63 ; vol. III, pp. 307–25.]

1872 MARSHALL, Alfred.   Review of Jevons's "Theory of
political economy." *Academy*, vol. I, no. 4.

1872 WITTSTEIN, T.   On mathematical statistics and its
application to political economy and insurance.
Jour. Instit. Actuaries (London), pp. 178–89.
[Continued, 1873, pp. 355–69, 417–35.]

1873 LEFÈVRE, H.   Physiologie et mécanique sociales.
Jour. des actuaires français, vol. II, pp. 211–
50, 351–88, Paris. [Continued, vol. III, pp.
93–118.]

1873 POCHET, Léon.   Géométrie des jeux de bourse.
Jour. des actuaires français, vol. II, pp. 153–60.

1874 AVIGDOR, S. N.   Question d'économie sociale.
Jour. des actuaires français, vol. III, pp. 300–6,
Paris.

1874 DORMOY, Émile.   Les matières premières, établisse-
ment des coefficients d'élaboration. *Jour. des
actuaires français*, vol. III, pp. 142–62, Paris.

1874 LEFÈVRE, H.   Principe de la science de la bourse.
Méthode approuvée par la chambre syndicale des
agents de change de Paris. Paris, 113 pp.

1875 FLEISCHHAUER, Oscar.   Theorie und Praxis der
Renteberechnung. Berlin (Weidmann), 815 pp.

1875 FONTANEAU, E.   Principes de chrématistique. *Jour.
des actuaires français*, vol. IV, pp. 75–83, 151–72.

o

[Continued, 1876, *ibid*, vol. V, pp. 70–96, 341–65.]

1875 LAURENT, H. Démonstration simple du principe de M. Menier. *Jour. des actuaires français*, vol. IV, pp. 84–7.

1881 EDGEWORTH, F. Y. Mathematical psychics. An essay on the application of mathematics to the moral sciences. London, viii, 150 pp.

1882 LAUNHARDT, Wilhelm. Der zweckmässigste Standort einer gewerblichen Anlage. *Zeitschr. des Vereins deutscher Ingen.*

1884 POYNTING, J. H. A comparison of the fluctuations in the price of wheat and in cotton and silk imports into Great Britain. *Jour. Statist. Soc.*, vol. XLVII, pp. 34–64.

1885 FAUVEAU, G. Les effets de la liberté du travail. *Jour. des écon.*, 4th ser., vol. XXXI, pp. 345–9.

1885 LEHR, Julius. Beiträge für Statistik der Preise, insbesondere des Geldes und des Holzes. Frankfurt.

1886 FAUVEAU, G. Études sur les premiers principes de la science économique. *Jour. des écon.*

1886 GROSSMANN, Ludwig. Die Mathematik im Dienste der Nationaloekonomie. I. Lief., Wien, 4°, 80 pp. [II. Lief., 1887 ; III, 1888 ; IV, 1889 ; V, 1890 ; VI, 1891 ; VII, 1895.]

1886 LEHR, Julius. Waldwertrechnung und Statistik. Handb. Forstwiss. Tübingen (Lorcy).

1887 AKIN-KAROLY. Solutions nouvelles de deux questions fondamentales d'économie sociale. *Rev. d'écon pol.* (Paris), vol. I, pp. 345–65.

1887 CHEYSSON, Émile. La statistique géométrique, *Jour. le génie civil* (Paris). [Also separately 37 pp.]

1887 EDGEWORTH, F. Y. Metretike, or the method of measuring probability and utility. London (Temple Co.).

1887 JANSON-DURVILLE, E. Cours de mathématique appliquée aux opérations financières. Paris.

1887 LEHR, Julius. Zur Statistik der Preise. *Zeitschr. Forst. und Jagdwesen.*

1888 LEHR, Julius. Eine Principienfrage der Forstwirtschaft. *Vierteljahrschr. für Volkswirtsch.*, Bd. XCIX, pp. 36–80, 143–71.

1889 BÖHM-BAWERK, Eugene. Positive Theorie des Kapitals. Innsbrück (Wagner). [Transl. into English (with preface and analysis) by Wm. Smart, London (Macmillan), 1891, xl, 428 pp. Appendix (2 pp.) math.]

1889 LAUNHARDT, Wilhelm. Die Ablösung der Baulasten und die Vergleichung der Bau Ausführungen in Materialien von verschiedener Dauer. *Zeitschr. des Hannover. architek. und ingen. Verein.*

1889 WICKSTEED, P. H. On certain passages in Jevons's "Theory of political economy." *Quart. Jour. Econ.*, Apr., pp. 293-314.

FROM MARSHALL TO THE PRESENT TIME

(1890-1897)

GENERAL TREATISES

1890 MARSHALL, Alfred. Principles of economics. Vol. I.
London (Macmillan), 770 pp. [2d ed., 1891 ;
3d ed., 1895.] [Math. footnotes and appendix.]

1890 PANTALEONI, Maffeo. Principi di economia pura.
Florence (Barbera), 16°, 376 pp.

1891 WESTERGAARD, Harald. Indledning til Studiet af
Nationaloekonomien. Copenhagen (Philipsen),
88 pp.

1892 FRANCKE, Adolf. Mathematische Grundlagen der
Wirthschaftslehre. Berlin (Ernst), 51 pp.

1892 PATTEN, S. N. The theory of dynamic economics.
Publicat. Univ. Penn. (Philadelphia), vol. III, no.
2, viii, 153 pp. [Slightly math.]

1892 PARETO, Vilfredo. Considerazioni sui principii fondamentali dell' economia politica pura. *Giorn. degli
econ*, May, pp. 389–420 ; June, pp. 485–512 ;
Aug., pp. 117–57. [Continued, 1893, Jan., pp.
1–37 ; Oct., pp. 279–321.]

1893 DEVINE, E. T. Economics. An elementary pres-
entation of the newer theories of production and
consumption. Philadelphia, 100 pp. [Slightly
math.]

1893 EFFERTZ, Otto. Katechismus der politischen Oeconomie, Basel (Müller), xii, 212 pp.

1893 LEHR, Julius. Grundbegriffe und Grundlagen der
Volkswirthschaft. Leipzig (Hirschfeld), xiv, 375

pp. [I. Abt., I. Bd. of Frankenstein's Hand- und Lehrbücher der Staatswiss.]

1896 HADLEY, A. T. Economics; an account of the relations between private property and public welfare. New York (Putnam), xi, 496 pp. [Slightly math.]

1896 PARETO, Vilfredo. Cours d'économie politique, professé à l'université de Lausanne. Lausanne (Rouge), vol. I, viii, 430 pp. [vol. II, 1897, 426 pp.]

1897 WALRAS, Léon. Études d'économie politique appliquée. (Théorie de la production de la richesse sociale.) [Contains : Théorie mathematique du billet de banque, 1879. *Bull. soc. vaudoise sci. nat.*, 1879 ; D'une methode de régularisation de la variation de valeur de la monnaie. *Ibid.*, 1885 ; Contribution à l'étude des variations des prix. [In collaboration with ALFRED SIMON.] *Ibid.*, 1885 ; Monnaie d'or avec billon d'argent regulateur. Brussels, 1884 ; Théorie de la monnaie. Lausanne, 1886, xii, 124 pp. Note sur la solution du problème monétaire anglo-indien. *Rev. d'écon. pol.*, 1887, p. 633. [Eng. transl., 1888, in *Rep't Brit. Assoc.* for 1887, p. 849.]

ON VALUE, TAXATION, AND DISTRIBUTION

Value

1890 JURISCH, Konrad W. Mathematische Diskussion des Entwickelungsgesetzes der Werterzeugung durch industrielle Produktionsgruppen. *Vierteljahrschr. Volkswirths., Polit. und Kulturgesch.* (Berlin), 27. Jahrg., Bd. III, pp. 46–84, 158–96.

1891 BERRY, Arthur.   Alcune brevi parole sulla teoria del baratto di A. Marshall. *Giorn. degli. econ.*, June, pp. 549–53. [Slightly math.]

1891 EDGEWORTH, F. Y.   La théorie mathématique de l'offre et de la demande et le coût de production. *Revue d'écon. pol.*, Jan.

1891 PATTEN, S. N.   Die Bedeutung der Lehre von Grenznutzen. *Jahrb. Nationaloek. u. Statist.*, 3ᵗᵉ Folge, Bd. II, pp. 481–534.

1892 CLARK, J. B.   The ultimate standard of value. *Yale Rev.*, vol. I, pp. 258–75.

1892 CUNYNGHAME, Henry.   Some improvements in simple geometrical methods of treating exchange value, monopoly, and rent. *Econ. Jour.*, vol. II, pp. 35–52.

1892 FISHER, Irving.   Mathematical investigations in the theory of value and prices. *Trans. Conn. Acad.* (New Haven), vol. IX, pp. 1–124.

1892 PARETO, Vilfredo.   La teoria dei prezzi dei Signori Anspitz e Lieben e le osservazioni del Professor Walras. *Giorn. degli econ.*, Mar.

1893 PATTEN, S. N.   Cost and expense. *Annals Amer. Acad. Polit. and Soc. Sci.*, vol. III, pp. 35–67.

1893 ROSS, E. A.   The total utility standard of deferred payments. *Annals Amer. Acad. Polit. and Soc. Sci.*, vol. IV, pp. 89–105. [Slightly math.]

1893 WICKSELL, Knut.   Ueber Wert, Kapital und Rente nach den neueren nationaloekonomischen Theorien. Jena (Fischer), xvi, 143 pp.

1893 ZUCKERKANDL, Robert.   Die statistische Bestimmung des Preisniveaus. Handwört. Staatswiss. (Jena), Bd. V, pp. 242–51. [Slightly math.]

1894   BARONE, Enrico.   A proposito delle indagini del
       Fisher.   *Giorn. degli econ.*, May, pp. 413–39.

1894   BARONE, Enrico.   Sulla "Consumer's Rent." *Giorn.
       degli econ.*, vol. IX, pp. 211–24.

1894   EDGEWORTH, F. Y.   Theory of international values.
       Econ. Jour., pp. 35–50, 424–43, 606–38.

1894   EDGEWORTH, F. Y.   Professor J. S. Nicholson, on
       "Consumer's rent." *Econ. Jour.*, vol. IV, pp.
       151–8.   [Slightly math.]

1894   PARETO, Vilfredo.   Il massimo di utilita dato dalla
       libera concorrenza.   *Giorn. degli econ.*, vol. IX,
       pp. 48–66.

1894   PARETO, Vilfredo.   Teoria matematica dei cambi
       forestieri.   *Giorn. degli econ.*, Feb., pp. 142–73.

1894   SCHRÖDER, H.   Der wirtschaftliche Wert.   Begriff und
       Normen.   Berlin (Puttkammer & Mühlbrecht),
       iv, 103 pp.   [Slightly math.]

1894   WICKSTEED, P. H.   Degree of utility.   Palgrave's
       Dict. pol. econ, London (Macmillan), vol. I, pp.
       536–7.   [Very slightly math.]

1895   FETTER, Frank.   The exploitation of theories of value
       in the discussion of the standard of deferred pay-
       ments.   *Annals Amer. Acad. Polit. and Soc. Sci.*,
       vol. V, pp. 882–96.   [Slightly math.]

1895   PARETO, Vilfredo.   La legge della domanda.   *Giorn.
       degli econ.*, vol. X, pp. 59–68.

1895   PARETO, Vilfredo.   Teoria matematica del com-
       mercio internazionale.   *Giorn. degli econ.*, Apr.,
       pp. 476–98.

1895   TAYLOR, W. G. L.   Some important phases in the
       evolution of the idea of value.   *Jour. Pol. Econ.*,
       vol. III, pp. 414–33.   [Slightly math.]

1896 WERNICKE, Johannes. Der objective Wert und
      Preis. Grundlegung einer reelen Wert und
      Preistheorie. Jena (Fischer), 116 pp. [Slightly
      math.]
1896 WICKSTEED, P. H. Final degree of utility. Pal-
      grave's Dict. pol. econ., London (Macmillan),
      vol. II, pp. 59–61.
1897 EDGEWORTH, F. Y. La teoria pura del monopolio.
      Giorn. degli econ., July, pp. 13–31.
1897 TAYLOR, W. G. L. Values, positive and relative.
      Ann. Amer. Acad. Polit. and Soc. Sci., Jan., pp.
      70–106.

Taxation

1892 SELIGMAN, E. R. A. On the shifting and incidence
      of taxation. *Publ. Amer. Econ. Assoc.*, vol. VII,
      nos. 2, 3. [Slightly math.]
1893 WEST, Max. The theory of the inheritance tax.
      Pol. Sci. Quart., vol. VIII, pp. 426–44. [Very
      slightly math.]
1894 BARONE, Enrico. Di alcuni teoremi fondamentali
      per la teoria matematica dell' imposta. *Giorn.
      degli econ.*, pp. 201–10.
1894 GROHMANN, E. Versuch einer stetig steigenden Scala
      für die progressive Einkommensteuer. *Zeitschr.
      für Volkswirtsch., Socialpolit. und Verwalt.*, vol.
      III, pp. 610–18.
1894 JOHNSON, E. R. Relation of taxation to monopo-
      lies. *Annals Amer. Acad. Polit. and Soc. Sci.*,
      vol. IV, pp. 68–93.
1895 KÖRNER, A. Indirecte Besteuerung und industrielle
      Technik in ihren Wechselbeziehungen. *Zeitschr.*

für Volkswirthsch., Socialpolit. und Verwalt., vol.
IV, pp. 193–235. [Slightly math.]

1896 CARVER, T. N. The shifting of taxes. *Yale Rev.*,
vol. V, pp. 258–71. [Slightly math.]

1896 WICKSELL, Knut. Finanztheoretische Untersuchungen nebst Darstellung und Kritik des Steuer-
wesens Schwedens. Jena (Fischer), xii, 352 pp.

1897 EDGEWORTH, F. Y. The pure theory of taxation.
Econ. Jour., vol. VII, pp. 46–70 ; pp. 226–38.

Distribution

1891 BERRY, Arthur. The pure theory of distribution.
Rept. Brit. Assoc. for 1890, pp. 923–4.

1891 HOBSON, John A. The law of the three rents.
Quart. Jour. Econ., vol. V, pp. 263–88.
[Slightly math.]

1891 JOHNSON, W. E. Exchange and distribution. Printed
by Cambridge [Eng.] Economic Club, 8 pp.

1892 LEHR, J. Die Durchschnittsprofitrate auf Grundlage
des Marx'schen Wertgesetzes. *Vierteljahrschr. für
Volkswirtsch.* (Berlin), Bd. CXIII, pp. 145–74 ;
Bd. CXIV, pp. 68–92.

1892 WICKSELL, Knut. Kapitalszins und Arbeitslohn.
Jahrb. Nationaloek. u. Statist., 3te Folge, Bd. VI,
pp. 852–74.

1893 CLARK, J. B. Surplus gains of labor. *Annals Amer.
Acad. Polit. and Soc. Sci.*, vol. III, pp. 79–89.

1893 COMMONS, J. R. The distribution of wealth. London (Macmillan), 258 pp. [Slightly math.]

1894 ANON. Examples showing the relation of the rate
of profit to surplus-value. *Jour. Pol. Econ.*,
vol. II, pp. 327–9.

1894 CARVER, T. N. The theory of wages adjusted to recent theories of value. *Quart. Jour. Econ.*, vol. VIII, pp. 377–402. [Math. note.]

1894 HOURWICH, I. A. Rate of profits under the law of labor-value. *Jour. Pol. Econ.*, vol. II, pp. 235–50.

1894 JOHNSON, W. E., and SANGER, C. P. On certain questions connected with demand. Printed by Cambridge [Eng.] Economic Club, 8 pp.

1894 KOMORZYNSKI, Joh. von. Thünen's naturgemässer Arbeitslohn. *Zeitschr. für Volksw., Socialpolit. und Verwalt.*, Bd. III, Heft I, pp. 27–62.

1894 WICKSTEED, P. H. Essay on the co-ordination of the laws of distribution. London (Macmillan), 56 pp.

1895 BEARDSLEY, Charles, Jr. The effect of an eight hours' day on wages and the unemployed. *Quart. Jour. Econ.*, vol. IX, pp. 450–9. [Slightly math.]

1895 CARVER, T. N. The ethical basis of distribution and its relation to taxation. *Annals Amer. Acad. Polit. and Soc. Sci.*, vol. VI, pp. 79–99. [Math. note.]

1895 LEXIS, Wilhelm. The concluding volume of Marx's Capital. *Quart. Jour. Econ.*, vol. X, pp. 1–33. [Very slightly math.]

1895 MOORE, H. L. Von Thünen's theory of natural wages. I. The classical theory and Von Thünen's formula. *Quart. Jour. Econ.*, vol. IX, pp. 291–303. II. Criticisms of the formula: natural wages $= \sqrt{AP}$. *Ibid.*, pp. 388–408.

1896 BARONE, Enrico. Studi sulla distribuzione; la prima approssimazione sintetica. *Giorn. degli. econ.*, Feb. and Mar.

1896 PARETO, Vilfredo. La courbe de la répartition de la richesse. (Extrait du recueil publié par la faculté de droit de l'université de Lausanne, à l'occasion de l'exposition nationale suisse. Genève, 1896, pp. 373-87.) Lausanne (Viret-Genton), 4°.

1896 PARETO, Vilfredo. La curva delle entrate e le osservazione del Professor Edgeworth. *Giorn. degli econ.*, vol. XIII, pp. 439-48.

1896 WALRAS, Léon. Études d'économie sociale. (Théorie de la répartition de la richesse sociale.) Lausanne (Rouge) & Paris (Pichon), viii, 464 pp. [Includes : Théorie mathématique du prix des terres et de leur rachat par l'état, *Bull. soc. vaudoise sci. nat.*, 1880.]

1897 BENINI, R. Di alcune curve descritte da fenomeni economici aventi relazione colla curva del reddito o con quella del patrimonio. *Giorn. degli. econ.*, Mar., pp. 177-214.

1897 EDGEWORTH, F. Y. La curva delle entrate e la curva di probabilità. *Giorn. degli econ.*, Mar., pp. 215-18. [Answered by Vilfredo Pareto, *ibid.*, pp. 219-20.]

1897 PARETO, Vilfredo. Aggiunta allo studio sulla curva delle entrate. *Giorn. degli econ.*, vol. XIV, pp. 15-26.

MISCELLANEOUS

Methodology

1892 EFFERTZ, Otto. Methodologie der politischen Oeconomie. Theil I, Wien (Seidl), iii, 92 pp.

1893   PATTEN, S. N. The scope of political economy. *Yale Rev.*, vol. II, pp. 264–87. [Very slightly math.]

1893   VOIGT, A.   Zahl und Mass in der Oekonomie, eine kritische Untersuchung der mathematischen Methode und der mathematischen Preisbildung. *Zeitschr. gesammte Staatsw.*, no. 4.

1894   EDGEWORTH, F. Y. Curves. Palgrave's Dict. pol. econ., London (Macmillan), vol. I, pp. 473–4.

1894   EDGEWORTH, F. Y. Demand curves. Palgrave's Dict. pol. econ., vol. I, pp. 542–4.

1894   EDGEWORTH, F. Y. Dupuit. Palgrave's Dict. pol. econ., vol. I, pp. 654–5. [Slightly math.]

1894   FLUX, A. W. Diagrams. Palgrave's Dict. pol. econ., vol. I, pp. 574–6.

1894   GROSSMANN, Ludwig. Compendium der praktischen Volkswirthschaft und ihrer mathematischen Disciplinen. Wien (Grossmann).

1896   EDGEWORTH, F. Y. Functions. Palgrave's Dict. pol. econ., vol. II, pp. 167–9.

1896   EDGEWORTH, F. Y. Gossen. Palgrave's Dict. pol. econ., vol. II, pp. 231–3.

1896   EDGEWORTH, F. Y. Least squares. Palgrave's Dict. pol. econ., vol. II, p. 587.

1896   PARETO, Vilfredo. Il modo di figurare i fenomeni economici. *Giorn. degli econ.*, vol. XII, pp. 75–87.

Money

1892   EDGEWORTH, F. Y. Recent attempts to evaluate the amount of coin circulating in a country. *Econ. Jour.*, pp. 162–9. [Slightly math.]

1892 ROSS, Edward A. Sinking funds. *Publ. Amer. Econ. Assoc.*, vol. VII, nos. 4 & 5, 106 pp. [Very slightly math.]

1893 HOXIE, R. F. The compensatory theory of bimetallism. *Jour. Pol. Econ.*, vol. I, pp. 273–6.

1894 FISHER, Irving. The mechanics of bimetallism. *Econ. Jour.*, vol. IV, pp. 527–37.

1894 NICHOLSON, J. S. The effects of the depreciation of silver, with special reference to the Indian currency experiment. *Econ. Jour.*, vol. IV, pp. 59–68. [Slightly math.]

1895 CLARK, J. B. The gold standard of currency in the light of recent theory. *Pol. Sci. Quart.*, vol. X, pp. 389–403. [Slightly math.]

1895 DES ESSARS, Pierre. La vitesse de la circulation de la monnaie. *Jour. soc. statist. de Paris*, pp. 143–52. [Ital. trans. *Giorn. degli. econ.* Slightly math.]

1895 EDGEWORTH, F. Y. Thoughts on monetary reform. *Econ. Jour.*, vol. V, Sept., pp. 434–51.

1896 EDGEWORTH, F. Y. A defence of index numbers. *Econ. Jour.*, vol. VI, pp. 132–42. [Slightly math.]

1896 EDGEWORTH, F. Y. Index Numbers. Palgrave's Dict. pol. econ., vol. II, pp. 384–7. [Slightly math.]

1896 FISHER, Irving. Appreciation and interest : a study of the influence of monetary appreciation or depreciation on the rate of interest, with applications to the bimetallic controversy and the theory of interest. *Publ. Amer. Econ. Assoc.*, vol. XI, no. 4, 100 pp. [Part I math.]

1896 LINDSAY. Die Preisbewegung der Edelmetallen. Jena (Fischer). [Slightly math.]

1896 SOLVAY, Ernest. Principe et raison d'être du compta-
      bilisme social. *Annales de l'institut des sci. soc.*
      (Brussels), 18 pp. [Slightly math.]
1896 ZAGNONI, Arturo.   Moneta e costi comparati.
   · *Giorn. degli econ.*, pp. 264–71.
1897 BOWLEY, A. L.   Import and export index-numbers.
      Econ. Jour., vol. VII, pp. 274–8.
1897 WICKSELL, Knut. Der Geldzins und die Warenpreise.
      Jena (Fischer). [Slightly math.]

                    Transportation

1890 COLSON, C.   Transports et tarifs. Paris (Rothschild),
      479 pp. [Slightly math.]
1890 LAUNHARDT, Wilhelm.   Theorie der Tarifbildung des
      Eisenbahnen. Berlin (Springer), viii, 84 pp.
1890 LILL, Eduard.   Das Preisgesetz und seine Anwend-
      ung auf den Eisenbahnverkehr. Wien (Spiel-
      hagen).
1891 LAUNHARDT, Wilhelm.   Die Zweckmässigste Höhe des
      Personenfahrgeldes auf den Eisenbahnen. *Zeitschr.*
      des Hannover. architek. und ingen. Verein.
1891 PARETO, Vilfredo.   Dell' utile che procurano al paese
      le ferrovie. *Giorn. degli econ.*, vol. IV, pp. 154–62.
1893 PEROZZO, Luigi.   Utilita differenziale delle ferrovia.
      Atti della Ra. Accad. dei Lincei, Jan.
1893 WEICHS, F. von.   Über das Wesen und die Grundlagen
      der Eisenbahn-Gütertarife. *Zeitschr. für die ge-*
      sammte Staatsw., pp. 42–97.
1894 COOLEY, C. H.   The theory of transportation. *Publ.*
   · *Amer. Econ. Assoc.*, vol. IX, 148 pp. [Very
      slightly math.]

1896 DE BENEDETTI. Costo delle ferrovie. *Giorn. della soc. degli ingegn.* Rome, 1896–97.

Unclassified

1890 CUGIN, E. Théorie et pratique de l'intérèt et de l'amortissement. Paris (Guillaumin).

1890 MARIE, Léon. Traité mathématique et pratique des opérations financières. Paris (Gauthier-Villars).

1890 VAUTHIER, L. L. Quelques considérations élémentaires sur les constructions graphiques et leur emploi en statistique. *Jour. soc. stat. de Paris*, 31st year, pp. 166–91. [Slightly math.]

1890 WESTERGAARD, Harald. Die Grundzüge der Theorie der Statistik. Jena (Fischer), vi, 286 pp. [pp. 202–24 economic.]

1890 X. Di alcuni errori di matematica che trovansi nell'opera del Prof. Loria "Analisi della proprietà capitalista. *Giorn. degli econ.*, Aug.

1891 EDGEWORTH, F. Y. Osservazioni sulla teoria matematica dell' economia politica con riguardo speciale ai Principi di economia di Alfredo Marshall. *Giorn. degli econ.*, Mar., pp. 233–45.

1891 JURISCH, K. W. Die Abhängigkeit zwischen Kapital und Zinsfuss. *Vierteljahrschrift für Volkswirtschaft* (Berlin), Bd. CXI, pp. 1–38.

1892 SCHULLERN-SCHRATTENHOFEN, Hermann von. Die Gesetzgebung über den Gläubiger-Concurs vom Standpunkte der Volkswirtschaft. *Zeitschr. für Volkswirtschaft, Socialpolitik und Verwaltung,* Bd. I, Heft 3, pp. 420–71. [Very slightly math.]

1892 Bilgram, Hugo. Comments on the Positive theory of capital. *Quart. Jour. Econ.*, vol. VI, pp. 190–206.

1892 Clark, J. B. Patten's Dynamic economics. *Annals Amer. Acad. Polit. and Soc. Sci.*, vol. III, pp. 30–44.

1892 Pareto, Vilfredo. Di un errore del Cournot nel trattare l'economia politica colla matematica. *Giorn. degli econ.*, Jan., pp. 1–14.

1893 Carver, T. N. The place of abstinence in the theory of interest. *Quart. Jour. Econ.*, vol. VIII, pp. 40–61.

1893 Helm, Georg. Eine Anwendung der Theorie des Tauschwerthes auf die Wahrscheinlichkeitsrechnung. *Zeitschr. Math. und Phys.* (Leipzig), pp. 374–6.

1893 Pareto, Vilfredo. La mortalita infantile e il costo dell' uomo adulto. *Giorn. degli econ.*, vol. VII, pp. 451–6.

1894 Barone, Enrico. Sur trattamento di quistioni dinamiche. *Giorn. degli econ.*, Nov., pp. 407–35.

1894 Clark, J. B. A universal law of economic variation. *Quart. Jour. Econ.*, vol. VIII, pp. 261–79.

1894 Edgeworth, F. Y. Average. Palgrave's Dict. pol. econ. London (Macmillan), vol. I, p. 74. [Very slightly math.]

1894 Lewis, W. D. The adaptation of society to its environment. *Annals Amer. Acad. Polit. and Soc. Sci.*, vol. IV, pp. 37–64. [Very slightly math.]

1894 Pareto, Vilfredo. Théorie mathématique des changes étrangers. *Assoc. franç. avanc. sci.*

1894 Wicksteed, P. H. Dimensions of economic quantities. Palgrave's Dict. pol. econ., vol. I, pp. 583–5.

1895 BARONE, Enrico. Sopra un libro del Wicksell. *Giorn. degli econ.*, Nov., 16 pp.

1895 SANGER, C. P. Recent contributions to mathematical economics. *Econ. Jour.*, vol. V., pp. 113–38.

1895 SANGER, C. P. The fair number of apprentices in a trade. *Econ. Jour.*, vol. V, pp. 616–36.

1895 HAYNES, John. Risk as an economic factor. *Quart. Jour. Econ.*, vol. IX, pp. 409–49. [Very slightly math.]

1895 YULE, G. U. On the correlation of total pauperism with proportion of outrelief. *Econ. Jour.*, vol. V, pp. 603–8 [continued, 1896, vol. VI, pp. 613–21].

1896 BIRCK, L. U. Konsumenter kontra Producenter. *Nationaloek. Tidsskrift*, pp. 419–41. [Slightly math.]

1896 CLARK, J. B. The unit of wealth. In Staatswiss. Arbeiten Festgaben für Karl Knies, pp. 3–20. Berlin (Haering). [Slightly math.]

1896 PATTEN, S. N. The theory of social forces. Suppl. to *Annals Amer. Acad. Polit. and Soc. Sci.*, Jan., pp. 1–151. [Very slightly math.]

1896 MONTEL, Enrico de. Le leggi dell' interesse Scansano (Olmi), 23 pp.

1896 WULFF, Julius. Have Forbrugere og Producenter modsatte Interesser? *Nationaloek. Tidsskrift*, pp. 596–621.

1897 FISHER, Irving. Senses of "capital." *Econ. Jour.*, vol. VII, pp. 199–213. [Very slightly math.]

1897 WICKSELL, Knut. Review of Vilfredo Pareto's Cours d'économie politique. Tome I. *Zeitschr. für Volkswirthschaft, Socialpolitik und Verwaltung*, Bd. VII. Heft I, p. 160. [Math. note.]

ᵖ

INDEX OF WRITERS

211

CPSIA information can be obtained at www.ICGtesting.com
Printed in the USA
LVOW072345290112

266127LV00005BA/159/P